IS THE CHURCH PARTIALLY RESPONSIBLE FOR THE BREAKUP OF THE HOME?

Dr. Eleazer Benenhaley

Order this book online at www.trafford.com/08-1142
or email orders@trafford.com

Most Trafford titles are also available at major online book retailers.

Note for Librarians: A cataloguing record for this book is available from Library and Archives Canada at www.collectionscanada.ca/amicus/index-e.html

ISBN: 978-1-4251-8643-2

We at Trafford believe that it is the responsibility of us all, as both individuals and corporations, to make choices that are environmentally and socially sound. You, in turn, are supporting this responsible conduct each time you purchase a Trafford book, or make use of our publishing services. To find out how you are helping, please visit www.trafford.com/responsiblepublishing.html

Our mission is to efficiently provide the world's finest, most comprehensive book publishing service, enabling every author to experience success. To find out how to publish your book, your way, and have it available worldwide, visit us online at www.trafford.com/10510

www.trafford.com

North America & international
toll-free: 1 888 232 4444 (USA & Canada)
phone: 250 383 6864 ♦ fax: 250 383 6804 ♦ email: info@trafford.com

The United Kingdom & Europe
phone: +44 (0)1865 487 395 ♦ local rate: 0845 230 9601
facsimile: +44 (0)1865 481 507 ♦ email: info.uk@trafford.com

10 9 8 7 6 5 4 3 2 1

FOREWARD

"The intriguing title, `Is the Church Partially Responsible for the BreakUp of the Home?' is Eleazer Benenhaley's question of the hour. Most people would instantly conclude that the church has nothing to do with the problems of the home. Benenhaley argues logically and persuasively that the church is one of the biggest culprits and calls us to once again proclaim the "whole counsel of God." This book may not make Benenhaley popular with very many people in the anything goes, postmodern climate, but if you care about what God's word clearly states, then this is an essential read by a wonderful man of God."

Paige Patterson
Southwestern Baptist Theological Seminary
Fort Worth, Texas

Dr. Benenhaley has done a careful and excellent exposition of what the Bible says about marriage, divorce, and intimate personal relationships. While it is aimed at an audience of ministers, seminarians, and seminary students, it is a must-read for anyone doing Christian marriage counseling.

T. Keith Edwards, M.D.

DEDICATION

Since this is a book about the family, I am dedicating it to my family! My mother, Hallie Benenhaley, is 92 years old. Life has been tough for her, but the Lord has seen her through many problems. She and my dad separated when they were 21 and neither of them ever remarried. Mom did her best to give me the best and I will always love her for her devotion to her Lord and me.

My precious wife, Nina, of 53 years, has been a constant guide and supporter all these years. What a supporter she has been these 50 years in the ministry. One deacon said to me, "The way you can preach, you could go somewhere if you had a personality like your wife." He was at least right about the "personality part." She had to be a good woman to put up with me, Clayton, Wilbur and Timothy. Clayton and Debra have given us Alexis, Meredith and Matthew as grandchildren. Alexis has given us a great-grandchild, Jada. Wilbur is divorced and helps me take care of my mother. Timothy and Tammy have given us three grandchildren, Breanna, Brooke, and Blair. Meredith and Matthew are twins and so are Breanna and Brooke.

It is my prayer that God will bless each member of my family and that each will walk in the ways of the Lord. I trust that each member of my family can say that Nina and I have been a Christian example to them.

CONTENTS

Foreward........iii
Dedication........iv
Contents........v
Acknowledgments........vi
Introduction........vii

The Home Is God's Design........1
Satan Seeks to Destroy the Home........6
Even after the Fall God Uses the Home for His Glory........10
God's Standards On Which to Build and Keep a Home........19
You Cannot Disobey God's Law and Not Get Hurt........31
God Solidified the Foundation of the Home By Sending His Blessed Son........41
What Are Some Historical Events Which Have Helped Weaken the Foundation of the Home?........47
Does the Bible Give Grounds for the Breakup of the Home?........64
What Can the Church Do, If Anything, to Strengthen Marriage and the Home?........71
What Part Does Repentance Play When God's Word Has Been Disobeyed?........80
The Home is Badly Battered Today, but God Is Still in the Restoration Business........96
What Insights Can Be Gleaned From This Study to Help Stem the Tragedy of Divorce?........109
When the Storms Come, Call Upon the Peacemaker........119
It Is Time for the Home to Be the Home........124

Endnotes........129
Biographical Sketch........133

ACKNOWLEDGMENTS

Mrs. Beverly Reece has been so helpful in typing and retyping the materials for this book. I will always be thankful for her tireless help. Beverly is a dear Christian friend.

Mrs. Kathleen Todd, an English teacher at North Augusta High School, read my manuscript and corrected my mistakes as well as offering helpful advice. I am thankful that Kathleen was willing to share her time and expertise!

Mrs. Lynn Burdette was so kind to type the final draft. She is so busy as the Financial Secretary of the Sweetwater Baptist Church, but was still willing to help me with this paper.

Dr. Keith Edwards, a retired Southern Baptist medical missionary and writer, has read and offered some helpful advice. I appreciate the friendship and prayers of this great man of God.

I am so thankful to the following publishers who allowed me to quote from their materials:

1. The United Educators, Inc.
2. The Center for Civic Education.
3. Christian Publishers, Inc.
4. Abingdon Press.

I take full responsibility for any mistakes in this book. May God use it to touch the life of a family.

INTRODUCTION

This Study is being done with the understanding that the majority will disagree with the writer's views and conclusions. But disagreement opens the door for dialogue and will cause those who disagree to rethink their own values and conclusions.

Controversy is not always bad, especially when it causes people to think! In a pluralistic and humanistic society like ours, what business does the church have in giving directions about home life? In fact, the church has become so diverse and divided until many will no longer seek her advice. Too many times, the church member's home life shows as much fracture and turbulence as do those who never attend church.

If the church has lost her respect and sense of responsibility, what is the cause or reason? Has pluralism invaded the church? Do church members believe that there are no "absolutes?" If there are no areas of black and white, but only gray areas, it is easy to see why people do just as they please. This is exactly what happened during the period of the Judges. "In those days there was no King in Israel, but every man did that which was right in his own eyes" (Judges 17:6, KJV). Humanistic philosophy is being taught in most of our educational systems. When our young people are taught that man is in control of his own destiny, who needs God, if there is one? Young people who sit under teachers who are atheistic and humanistic are in more danger than our young people who are sent off to fight terrorists. The danger to our homes and churches is not "over there," but "right here."

If I sound frustrated almost to the point of anger, I am! Some who read my suggestions and conclusions will think of me as being cold and uncaring. That assumption would be far from the truth. I am writing from the background of over forty years as a pastor. I have witnessed the pain of those whose homes have been destroyed by Satan. I know the pain of coming from a broken home myself. My wife and I have hurt with two of our sons as they went through the heartache of divorce.

From the world's standpoint, the cards are stacked against the home. Yet, there is still hope. If biblical standards are taught and followed, our homes can be saved.

Something is tragically wrong when couples can get a divorce for "incompatibility." Couples can just agree that they will not live together anymore, and the states will grant a divorce. Pastors will remarry couples even when there are no biblical grounds at all. Their reasons being, "if I don't do it, they will go to a Justice of the Peace" or "maybe I will be able to minister to them." Both reasons are flawed! Being married by a minister will not make a wrong right. A minister cannot disobey God's Word and expect to have an effective ministry with anyone. It is not uncommon for a person to be married in the church multiple times. Does a pastor have a right to be disobedient to the Bible in order to please some member? What kind of witness will a church have when she willfully condones something that is in opposition to God's Word?

What can the church do, if anything, to stem the erosion and breakup of the home? In the Old Testament, the prophets were God's mouth piece to the nation and to the home. In the New Testament, Jesus called His disciples to be His mouth piece. Matthew 16:18 tells about the importance of the church. If the home is destroyed, the church is devastated. Something needs to be done to fix the problem. It is my belief that God called, obedient pastors, are the key to our homes being restored. It is not easy to stand against the tide, especially when one feels alone. God has had his man in the past and He has those today who can make a difference (Ezekiel 22:30). Ezekiel was the one man who stood for God in his day when the majority disobeyed. There must be a return to the Bible as our guidebook (Psalms 115:105; Proverbs 6:23). God's standards rather than man's standards must be taught in our churches. Before young people are engaged to be married, they should be taught the permanency of marriage according to the Word of God (Psalms 127:1). By the time they are engaged, their minds are already made up, even though, they are not for each other.

As has already been stated, pastors must get their instructions and guidelines about marriage from the Bible rather than from the prevailing view of the world. It must be understood that rules for marriage, in and outside of the church, must be according to God's standards. It is alarming that many who call themselves conservatives find more reasons to divorce and remarry than do liberal scholars.

Let's take a fair and honest look through the Bible and see what is said about the home. Let's look at God's plan for the home and see whose beliefs are correct; God's or men. It is possible that through this study some insights might be gained as to when the home began to crack and crumble. In today's world, man has devised ways to stop cracks and erosion. It would be a foolish person who would refuse to use proper methods to stop erosion around his home. Since God has given, in His Word, methods to keep the home safe and secure, it certainly is folly to refuse to use those methods. The big question for pastors of churches is, will there be obedience to the Word of God no matter the cost? If the pastors are obedient to the Word of God, what course will the churches take? When and if the pastors and churches accept God's standards for the home, how can pastors and churches in different locations work together to strengthen the home? Some suggestions will be given in a later chapter as to how this can be done. John says in John 8:32 "And ye shall know the truth, and the truth shall make you free." These powerful words are so needed today. Man's philosophy is to do what he thinks is best for him. But, if we are under the Lordship of Christ, His best for us is not always what we think is best. Many times, our understanding of what is right and wrong does not come from a correct understanding and application of the Bible. Paul makes this very clear in I Corinthians 2:14:

> But the natural man receiveth not the things of the Spirit of God: for they are foolishness unto him: neither can he know them, because they are spiritually discerned.

My reason for this study is to help young people, families, pastors, and churches to come back to an understanding of the purposes of the home and how to be obedient to God's guidelines. If people will allow God, to direct and control their lives, the erosion of the home will be stopped and God will be praised.

In such a study, we must begin where God begins with the home. we must look at His design and purpose. Since God's beginning for the home was perfect (mature), what has gone wrong to cause all the brokenness and pain today? We must not take scripture out of context, but compare scripture with scripture and see if God's design for the home has changed. We must look at why and at what theologians have to say about the home. In fact, we will see that some secular writers have a better grasp of the broken home problems than do some religious writers. After we take an honest look at God's design for the home and see what has gone wrong, we must be willing to correct what is destroying our homes.

Chapter I

The Home is God's Design

Genesis 1:1 says: "In the beginning God created the heaven and the earth." What man believes about this verse will determine what he believes about everything else God has to say. If God is sovereign, and He is, He has every right to plan man's itinerary. Paul says in Romans 8:28:

> And we know that all things work together for good to them that love God, to them who are called according to *his* purpose.

It is wonderful to know that before the world was ever formed God had a plan for man. The only way God's plan for man could be altered was for man to seek his own way.

One of the greatest verses in the entire Bible is Genesis 2:7:

> And the Lord formed man out *of* the dust of the ground, and breathed into his nostrils the breath of life; and man became a living soul.

There is no theologian who can explain all that is contained in that verse of scripture. When the Psalmist thought about the majesty of God, he asked this question, "What is man, that thou art mindful of him? and the son of man, that thou visitest him" (Psalms 8:4)?

David had been blessed with a good home. He had seen God's handiwork in his own life. He acknowledged his thankfulness when he said in Psalms 139:14:

> I will praise thee: for I am fearfully *and* wonderfully made: marvelous *are* thy works; and *that* my soul knoweth right well.

In Genesis 2:7, the words "life" and "living" are so full of power and expectation. Adam could enjoy all that God had provided for him. He could really say, "This is what life is all about." But what was next? What would this God who spoke the world into being, out of nothing, do next? He created a man out of the dust and exalted him to a place of leadership and authority. What would God do next? Our God is a God of surprises. Since God created Adam, He had a right to do with him and for him as He pleased or willed. Genesis 2:21-22 says:

> And the Lord God caused a deep sleep to fall upon Adam, and he slept: and he took one of his ribs, and closed up the flesh instead thereof; And the rib, which the Lord God had taken from man, made he a woman, and brought her unto the man.

When Adam awoke from his sleep, he could not believe what he saw. Standing before him was the most gorgeous creature he had ever seen. He had seen the many different animals God had created, but he had never seen anything like what was standing before him. He knew he had been asleep, but what was standing before him was no evolutionary process. This had to be God's work! The amazing thing for Adam was that God gave this beautiful creature--woman to him.

One must wonder what a different world we would have, if in our schools, universities and seminaries the Biblical creation event was taught. But no, most places of higher learning teach that out of a "big bang" explosion came water, an amoeba, followed by a tadpole, frog, ape and then man. No wonder there are those who want to replace Eve with a man and Adam with whatever. I think Adam would have been very disappointed had God presented him with another man instead of Eve. The two were very different, but very compatible.

It must be noted that Eve was brought to Adam by God. This is the beginning of the home. Since the home is by God's design, He should set the rules and standards. If man is not willing to be obedient to God's standards, why claim to be under His Lordship?

Today people use the word covenant and contract, when the term marriage is used. As a result, according to them, if either member breaks the covenant or contract, it sets the other person free. This notion blends right in with humanistic ideas, but it misses the mark biblically. When I go through the marriage vows, I always have the couple say, "Until death do us part." I cannot recall a wedding that I have attended where the words "until death do us part" were not used. On my own marriage certificate are these words from Mark 10:9: "What therefore God has joined together, let not man put asunder." Before two people agree to marry, they should understand the meaning of commitment and responsibility. If either one is not willing to stick to both terms, the marriage is doomed.

Adam accepted the permanency of marriage when he said: "… this is now bone of my bones, and flesh of my flesh: she shall be called Woman, because she was taken out of Man" (Genesis 2:23).

His statement is literally true, because Eve was actually a part of Adam's body; therefore, in a spiritual sense, when two give themselves to each other in marriage they become "one." Listen to those who say, "I am not willing to give up my individuality and freedom." Such remarks miss the point, but may suggest that the person or persons are not ready for marriage. Selfishness has no place in marriage. To be one, means to put self aside in order to honor and please one's mate. To be one, means a togetherness that seeks the will of God in making the home what God intended it to be. When two people surrender themselves to the Lordship of Christ, what it means to be "one" will become clearer as they walk in obedience to the Lord. Paul says in Galatians 2:20:

> I am crucified with Christ: nevertheless I live; yet not I, but Christ liveth in me: and the life which I now live in the flesh I live by the faith of the Son of God, who loved me, and gave himself for me.

Yes, being one has its mystery, as does being crucified with Christ, but by faith and obedience, every day should be a blessed day in Christ. Marriage is a beautiful picture of Christ and the church. Paul in

Ephesians 5:21-33 shows how both can have the victory. When a marriage is begun with both parties surrendered to God, the tools necessary for a life-fulfilling journey will be in place. The same can be said of the person who is crucified with Christ. Now that two people have become one, any attempt to tear them apart will bring pain and agony.

Before a person gets married, he or she must decide to give up one home in order to begin another home. An eagle will let her young stay in the nest for a time. But in due time, the eagle will push the eaglet out of the nest. This must be a frightening time for the young eagle. It is also a frightening time when two people decide to give up the freedom and comfort provided by mom and dad to start their own home. Genesis 2:24 gives a powerful admonition:

> Therefore shall a man leave his father and mother, and shall cleave unto his wife; and they shall be one flesh.

It is not good for a healthy young person to always depend upon his parents. For most people, there is that God-given desire to develop the abilities given by God. It is also natural for most young men to have a desire to share that life and development with a young woman who is the love of his life. The day finally comes when a young couple, trusting God, cuts the ties with their parents and begins their new life together. This young couple should not allow, nor expect, their parents to rule their home. Each group will have enough to do at their own home. Parents should be mature and wise enough to leave the young couple alone. There will be times, just as when the mother eagle was watchful and ready to lend a helpful wing, but the young couple must learn to fly on their own. Many young couples have never learned to provide for and keep a home because of over protecting parents. Many homes are destroyed because when problems arise, the wife is on the phone with the mother or the mother with the daughter. Young couples should work out their problems without meddling from their parents.

The admonition in Genesis 2:24 "to cleave" is a great word. Webster's dictionary says the word means to "cling," be "faithful," and to "stick." Divorce would be radically reduced if couples would cling rather than split. Just think what faithfulness to the wedding vows would do in times of adversity. What a difference there would be when pressures of the world seek to tear couples apart, if they would cleave and stick together no matter the circumstances.

Chapter II

Satan Seeks to Destroy the Home

Many people might wonder why Satan used the serpent to trick Eve. Genesis 3:1 answers that question by saying the serpent was more "subtle" than the other animals. Satan knew when and how to approach his foes. God allows Satan certain powers and one can be sure that Satan will use those powers to his advantage. This serpent, because of his beauty, evidently, got Eve's attention very quickly. Paul says to the Corinthians: "And no marvel; for Satan himself is transformed into an angel of light" (II Corinthians 11:14). The serpent began to work on Eve's mind. He wanted to plant a seed of doubt. He wanted her to believe that God did not have her best interest in mind. This is Satan's trick today and many, including leaders of the church, have swallowed his lie "hook, line, and sinker." Satan wants man to deny the sovereignty of God. If God is not sovereign, He cannot be holy and if He is not holy, His Word cannot be trusted. Since God does not mean what He says, man does not have to obey what He says. Satan's next lie is: "If God really loves you, you won't have to worry about any judgment." There are many who are teaching that disobedience does not have any consequences. Eve found out that a beautiful fruit brought ugly results. Many lives have been destroyed by reaching for fruits that appear exciting and beautiful. Delilah was beautiful and provided Samson a delightful time, but she cost him his eyes and life (Judges 16:21-31). Bathsheba was beautiful and David enjoyed a sin-filled time with her, but it cost him his joy and his family (II Samuel 12). Genesis 3:6-7 says:

<u>Divorce</u> would be radically reduced if couples would cling rather than split.

> And when the woman saw that the tree *was* good for food, and that it *was* pleasant to the eyes, and a tree to be desired to make *one* wise, she took of the fruit thereof, and did eat, and gave also unto her husband with her; and he did eat. And the eyes of them both were opened, and they knew that they *were* naked; and they sewed fig leaves together, and made themselves aprons.

Eve's disobedience brought pain and death to her family and opened the door to heartache, pain and death to all who were to follow. Yes, their "eyes" were opened and they saw and experienced things, which God never intended for them to see and experience. All of the blessings God had provided for Adam and Eve were lost in a moment of disobedience. Now the blame game begins. It is easy to ask why God allowed this to happen. Since God is sovereign and all knowing, He knew Eve would fail. Why did He let it happen? I certainly do not presume to know the great heart and mind of God, but I do know that He did not create us as robots. He created us as rational and responsible beings. Just as God wanted Adam to have fellowship with Eve, He wanted to have fellowship with them both. He wanted their fellowship to be a result of love and obedience.

Never before had Adam and Eve run from God. But never before had they sinned against God.

Never before had Adam and Eve run from God. But never before had they sinned against God. Adam and Eve knew they had been disobedient. This disobedience caused them to hide from God. Adam and Eve learned what people today need to learn; one cannot sin and hide from God. Notice that Eve blames the serpent, and Adam blames Eve. We must always remember that Eve was deceived, but not so with Adam. Listen to what God said to Adam in Genesis 2:15-17:

> And the Lord God took the man, and put him in the garden of Eden to dress it and to keep it. And the Lord God commanded the man, saying, Of every tree of the

> garden thou mayest freely eat: But of the tree of the knowledge of good and evil, thou shalt not eat of it: for in the day that thou eatest thereof thou shalt surely die.

Adam, in failing to take the leadership role in the home, allowed pain to enter his home and that pain is still with us today. I wonder how many times Adam and Eve discussed and wondered about the tree of the knowledge of good and evil? In the very beginning, God put man in a place of leadership. Adam was created first and Eve was made from his rib. It is natural to assume that Eve was to be under the leadership and protection of her husband. As we travel through scripture and early history, man was always in the leadership role, and when he was not, trouble arose. If man does not take his rightful place of leadership in the home, church, and state, things will not be as they should.

If man does not take his rightful place in the home, church, and state, things will not be as they should.

Every time I see a snake slither across the ground, it reminds me of Genesis 3:14. For the majority of people, snakes are an enemy. Let's take a good look at what Genesis 3:14-15 has to say:

> And the Lord God said unto the serpent, Because thou hast done this, thou *art* cursed above all cattle, and above every beast of the field; upon thy belly shalt thou go, and dust shalt thou eat all the days of thy life: And I will put enmity between thee and the woman, and between thy seed and her seed; it shall bruise thy head, and thou shalt bruise his heel.

Many scholars believe that Geneses 3:15 is the first mention of redemption and victory over the old serpent. Satan will deceive many but God has made a way of escape through Jesus Christ (John 3:16).

Because of disobedience, Eve and women who have followed have brought children into the world through sorrow and pain. It will be woman's natural desire to please man, and he will be her leader. Children are brought into the world by much pain, but look at the joy a newborn brings into a home. There are those who think of man's leadership role as being dictatorial, but for the woman who loves and respects her husband, it is security and protection. God can bring good out of what seems to be so bad.

How many times has a person said, when toiling under the hot sun, or digging up rocks, or stuck by a thorn, "How I wish that Adam had not sinned?" Too many times, we fail to recognize that we are responsible for our actions today. When there is a broken relationship, Adam is not at fault. Adam and Eve started the problem, but ultimately each person is responsible for his own disobedience. Adam started the sin problem, but there is forgiveness through Jesus Christ (Romans 5:12-21). Yes, Adam's sin brought thorns, rocks, pain, and death, but Jesus Christ brought life (John 3:16). Praise God, by the grace of God a man can turn a rocky, briar-infested field into a beautiful field of fruit and homes. I am not sure that any man loves to break his back, blister his hands or toil all day under the scorching sun. However, where the love of God is, the hard work is soon forgotten as a man is surrounded by a loving family. Satan is a dangerous enemy and can cause much hurt and pain, but God provides healing and safety for those who will obey Him.

After God pronounced His judgment in the Garden of Eden, He showed His love for sinners. Genesis 3:21 reads: "Unto Adam also and to his wife did the Lord God make coats of skins and clothed them." In order for them to be covered, an animal had to die. Blood had to be shed. In order for man to be covered today, a perfect lamb had to die. That is exactly why the Lord Jesus died for our sins. The storms of Satan blew in on the first family and they were marred and bruised as a result. But by the grace and forgiveness of God, the first home survived. Adam and Eve raised children and cared for them and Adam lived to be 930 years old. By God's grace, mercy and forgiveness, families can make it today. There will be briars, thorns, and sweat and man can leave the fields as they are or he can, by God's help, turn the fields into a beautiful garden of herbs and flowers.

Chapter III

Even After the Fall God Uses the Home for His Glory

In the very beginning of history, there were those who served and honored God, while others lived lives of disobedience to God. Common sense dictates that it is unwise for those who serve God to marry those who do not. Yet, this is exactly what happened in Noah's day. As a result, God's patience ran out with man. Look at Genesis 6:5-7:

> And God saw that the wickedness of man *was* great in the earth, and *that* every imagination of the thoughts of his heart *was* only evil continually. And it repented the Lord that he had made man on the earth, and it grieved him at his heart. And the Lord said, I will destroy man whom I have created from the face of the earth; both man, and beast, and the creeping thing, and the fowls of the air; for it repenteth me that I have made them.

The people in Noah's day found out that God's way was the best way even though it was too late for most of them.

The happenings of history should be a guide, as well as, a warning to mankind. From the first chapter of Genesis through chapter 6, it is plain to see that disobedience brings God's judgment. As we study the Old Testament, God's prophets continually shamed the people because they did not learn from the blessings and mistakes of their fathers. Hopefully, as we look at the past and the present, we will understand that God's ways are the best. The people of Noah's day found out that God's way was the best way even though it was too late for most of them.

When all seemed hopeless, God found a man who was faithful. His name was Noah. Genesis 6:8-9 points out why Noah could be used by God. "He found grace in the eyes of the Lord; he was just and walked with God." If men today walked with God as Noah did, we would not have broken homes, which are so prevalent today. Noah was asked by God to do a task, which seemed impossible. He was asked to build a boat big enough to house animals and people to replenish the earth after God's judgment upon the earth. Evidently, Noah had a good relationship with his family. One would have to assume that his sons helped him build the ark.

In God's own time, Noah and his family entered into the ark. The rain and flood of forty days and nights destroyed all upon the earth, save Noah and his family. Even in the midst of judgment, God took care of His own. When the judgment was over, "God remembered Noah and his family." As we study Bible history, it seems fair to say that Noah's sons Shem, Ham, and Japheth were the fathers of the three great races that we have upon the earth today. The people were finally scattered to all parts of the earth when they tried to build Babel's tower to Heaven. It did not take these people long to find out that they could not become like God or take over His work. This is a lesson that today's world must learn. God chose Noah and his family in order that today's family can walk with Him.

In the darkest of times, God always finds someone who will obey Him and be a leader to mankind

In the darkest of times, God always finds someone who will obey Him and be a leader to mankind. Abraham was such a man. He was not always obedient and God often had to remind him of his call and place in history. All people, who believe the Bible, and those who do not, would do well to read and analyze Genesis 12:1-3:

> Now the Lord had said unto Abram, Get thee out of the country, and from thy kindred, and from they father's house, unto a land that I will shew thee: And I will make of thee a great nation, and I will bless thee, and make thy name great; and thou shalt be a blessing: And I will bless

> them that bless thee, and curse him that curseth thee: and in thee shall all families of the earth be blessed.

God's call to Abram was to go and not ask questions as to his destination. He was to become a great nation and a blessing to the world. There is a blessing in store for those who honor Abram and his people, but a curse upon those who do not. As America and her allies seek ways to bring peace to the Middle East, Genesis 12:3 should be the most important guide for any decisions that are made.

Abram appeared to be very close to his family. Although he had no children of his own, he took his brother's son, Lot, with him. As one reads through the Old Testament, he will see that people married within their own families. In fact, Sarai was Abram's half sister. This type of relationship would be unlawful today. What Abram did when he entered the land of the Egyptians, makes one wonder how much he loved and respected his wife, Sarai. In fact, by reading the story, it seems that Abram put his own safety ahead of Sarai's safety. Sarai was a beautiful woman and the Egyptian Pharaoh, according to the culture of that day, could take any woman he wanted! Evidently, Abram knew the culture and told his wife what to do. Sarai could have refused Pharaoh, but it would have meant death for both of them. Genesis 12:17 shows God's displeasure with what Pharaoh did:

Just because we read the Bible, pray and attend church is no guarantee that sin will not tempt us.

> And the Lord plagued Pharaoh and his house with great plagues because of Sarai, Abram's wife.

In the end, Pharaoh had more honor than did Abram. Before we condemn the Egyptian culture for allowing multiple wives, we had better examine the divorce rate in America. "But the law allows divorce in America," some would say. It appears the Egyptian law did also. But, was God pleased then and is He pleased now? God is so good. Even in the midst of disobedience, He protected Abram and Sarai. There is a lesson in this story, which should catch our attention. Just because we read the Bible, pray and attend church, is no guarantee that sin will not trap us. Just before Abram lied to Pharaoh, he had met with God and built an altar at Bethel. Bethel was to become a special place for people to call upon God.

The Importance Of Strong Family Ties

From what we have learned about Abram, thus far, his early family training was one of helpfulness. This can be seen by his patience with Lot. Lot was Abram's selfish and greedy nephew. When it became obvious that Abram and Lot could not dwell together, Abram allowed Lot the first choice of the land around them. Genesis 13:10-11 shows the kind of person Lot was:

> And Lot lifted up his eyes, and beheld all the plain of Jordan, that it *was* well watered every where, before the Lord destroyed Sodom and Gomorrah, *even* as the garden of the Lord, like the land of Egypt, as thou comest unto Zoar. Then Lot chose him all the plains of Jordan; and Lot journeyed east: and they separated themselves the one from the other.

Genesis 13:12-13 shows the tragic mistakes of Lot:

> Abram dwelled in the land of Canaan, and Lot dwelled in the cities of the plain, and pitched *his* tent toward Sodom. But the men of Sodom *were* wicked and sinners before the Lord exceedingly.

Lot was very fortunate to have an uncle like Abram. Genesis chapters 14 and 15 show how God used Abram to deliver sinful Lot. The entire chapter in Genesis 19 shows to what low depths of sin Lot and his family had fallen. Lot had chosen to bring his family up in the midst of sodomites (homosexuals). Verse 6 of chapter 19 makes it plain who these people were when it says: "that we might know them." This word "know" means to have sexual relations. In our day, there are those who accept such a lifestyle and demand that others accept it also. God showed that He did not accept such sinful practices by destroying the cities. Lot had so compromised with the life styles of those who lived around him until his family members and their friends had lost all respect for him. In fact, when Lot warned them about God's coming judgment, they made fun of him. His married daughters perished in the judgment. Listen to what Genesis 19:14 has to say:

> And Lot went out, and spake unto his sons in law, which married his daughters, and said, Up, get you out of this place; for the Lord will destroy this city. But he seemed as one that mocked unto his sons in law.

By compromising with sin, Lot lost his witness for good to his family and those around him. Greed and selfishness blinded him as to the dangerous road when he "pitched his tent towards Sodom."

What Does The Destruction Of Sodom And Gomorrah Say To America?

Has God changed His mind about the home? It is clear from scripture that the home began with a man and woman. Under the plans of God, children were to be born into that home. The people of Sodom and Gomorrah had attempted to change God's plan and were doing that which was unnatural (homosexuality). God destroyed those cities because of their sinful practices. Is America headed for God's judgment? There are those in America who do not want the name of Jesus mentioned or God's laws placed in public places. Yet, these same people want deviant behavior (alternate lifestyles) to have the same rights and privileges as do regular families. These same groups want homosexuality to be accepted in our schools and churches. If these people have their way, our families will cease to be, because no children will be born! It is easy to talk about God's blessing and the need to pray, but where there is blatant sin, it does not do any good to pray until there is repentance for that sin. Listen to what God says to Joshua in Chapter 7:10-11:

> And the Lord said unto Joshua, Get thee up; wherefore liest thou thus upon thy face? Israel hath sinned, and they have also transgressed my covenant which I commanded them: for they have even taken of the accursed thing, and have also stolen, and dissembled also, and they have put *it* even among their own stuff.

The godless teaching of homosexuality is against human nature, the Bible and everything God intended the home to be. If our homes, churches and states allow the radical teachings of the homosexuals to be accepted as a natural or alternate lifestyle, our country is headed for the judgment of God.

When a man is eighty-six and his wife is seventy-six, it is only natural that they would give up any hope of having a child together.

In some ways, Abram is not a strong example of a godly leader in the home. It must be understood that the law had not been given in his day. Neither did he have the Bible as we do today. However, Abram cannot be excused for his many lapses in judgment. But still, it helps us to know that Abram was human, sinned and was still used by God. Genesis 15:4-6 shows how God continued to mold and reshape Abram:

> And, behold, the word of the Lord *came* unto him, saying, This shall not be thine heir; but he that shall come forth out of thine own bowels shall be thine heir. And he brought him forth abroad, and said, Look now toward heaven, and tell the stars, if thou be able to number them: and he said unto him, So shall thy seed be. And he believed in the Lord: and he counted it to him for righteousness.

The Tragedy of Not Waiting On God

When a man is eighty-six and his wife is seventy-six, it is only natural that they would give up any hope of having a child together. It is always a dangerous thing to run ahead of God. It seems, according to the customs in Canaan, what Sarai does in Genesis 16:1-4 is legal and accepted by society. How "accepted by society" rings a bell today. When Sarai gave Hagar to Abram as his wife, he did not object at all. He went in to her and she gave him a son, Ishmael. In our day of broadmindedness, liberalism, and wife swapping, what is wrong with what Abram did, especially since it was okay with his wife? Such demon inspired thinking, is what is destroying our homes, churches and world. Jesus is the only way such things and actions can be changed.

From that very day, Abram's disobedience brought strife into his home. Sarai received a son, but Hagar was despised in her eyes from then on. The hatred, killing and division between the Arabs and Jews can be traced right back to the failure of Abram and Sarai to wait on God. Even after this disobedience, God changed Abram's name to Abraham and promised that he would be a "father of many nations" (Genesis 17:5). God changed Sarai's name to Sarah, and Abraham laughed when he was told that he was to have a son (Genesis 17:15-19). When you think of it, there probably were not many one hundred year-old fathers and ninety year-old mothers. That is, who has children born to them at that age? Sarah also laughed when she was told that she was to have a son (Genesis 18:12-3). It appears that Abraham and Sarah had forgotten that they were serving a God of miracles. The messenger of God asked a pointed question in Genesis 18:14:

> Is anything to hard for the Lord? At the time appointed I will return unto thee, according to the time of life, and Sarah shall have a son.

God's ways are not easy to understand. Our job is not to question, but to obey. God had brought Abraham through many adversities but none like offering his own son as a sacrifice. How could God give

Abraham and Sarah a son and then take him away? Look at the command of God and the obedience of Abraham as given in Genesis 22:2-3:

> And he said, take now thy son, thine only *son* Isaac, whom thou lovest, and get thee into the land of Moriah; and offer him there for a burnt offering upon one of the mountains which I will tell thee of. And Abraham rose up early in the morning, and saddled his ass, and took two of his young men with him, and Isaac his son, and clave the wood for the burnt offering, and rose up, and went unto the place of which God had told him.

God's Man Proved Himself Faithful

When God told Abram to leave his people and travel to a foreign land, he obeyed. God had to do some pruning to get Abram, later Abraham, in shape for service. Abraham in some ways is a type of God. This can be seen, as he is willing to offer his son as a sacrifice. Isaac is a type of the Lord Jesus as he obediently becomes a sacrifice. This young man could have gotten away from his father, but he was obedient through it all. Matthew 26:42 records how Jesus was obedient to his Father when he said:

> O my Father, if this cup may not pass away from me, except I drink it, thy will be done.

When Isaac was about to be slain, God provided the sacrifice (the ram caught in the thicket) just in time. Read Genesis 22:13-14:

> And Abraham lifted up his eyes, and looked, and, behold, behind *him* a ram caught in a thicket by his horns: and Abraham went and took the ram, and offered him up for a burnt offering in the stead of his son. And Abraham

> called the name of that place Jehovah-jireh: as it is said to this day, In the mount of the Lord it shall be seen.

Abram, with all of his failures, saw his home survive. Why? Because he learned obedience and how to walk with God. When problems came to his home, he did not bail out and run.

Adam and Eve paid an awful price for disobedience, and the results of disobedience is still with us today. But through all of the failures, God still took care of them. Their home survived.

Noah and his family were tested by God, but they were faithful. As a result of their faithfulness, we are allowed to be here today.

Throughout the Old Testament, God used His prophets to warn His people against disobedience. The sins of Abraham and Sarah show how God's grace and mercy were extended in the most difficult situations. The struggles of Abraham and his family give hope for today's family. Just as God pruned, chastised and protected Abraham and his family, God will do the same today.

In the book of Genesis, we see the beginning of the home, as well as the foundation and rooms. If we are not careful, we will just see the mistakes and problems, and not the growth and learning processes. It is amazing to see fallen creatures respond to the grace and leadership of God. Each family that has been studied faced enough difficulties with each other to leave and go their separate ways. But they stuck it out and weathered the storms. How were they able to survive? Each family that has been studied, even with their failures and disobedience, returned to God who sustained and protected them.

Chapter IV

God's Standards on Which to Build and Keep a Home

It is doubtful if there has ever been a home where jealousy did not abound. This is evident in the lives of children, youth and adults. Joseph is a model of stickability and perseverance. Genesis 37:2-4 shows what jealousy can do when it says:

> These are the generations of Jacob. Joseph, *being* seventeen years old, was feeding the flock with his brethren; and the lad *was* with the sons of Bilhah, and with the sons of Zilpah, his father's wives: and Joseph brought unto his father their evil report. Now Israel loved Joseph more than all his children, because he *was* the son of his old age: and he made him a coat of *many* colours. And when his brethren saw that their father loved him more than all his brethren, they hated him, and could not speak peaceably unto him.

It must be noted here that Israel had more than one wife (verse 2) and this resulted in a "blended family." There will be those who are quick to say, God had not said that a man could not have more than one wife; plus this was the "practice of the day." I must point out that God in Genesis 2:22 gave Adam one woman. Adam further stated in Genesis 2:24 "that a man was to cleave unto his wife," not wives!

Genesis chapter 31 shows what hatred can do in and to a family

To do an in-depth study of the life of Joseph, would take too much time for study here, but a survey of the important events and how they relate to the family will be used. It is exciting to see how God protects Joseph and Joseph's response to God's leadership.

Genesis chapter 31 shows what hatred can do in and to a family. Joseph's brothers' hatred had risen to the point of committing murder. Ruben talks the brothers into placing Joseph in a pit with the idea of releasing him later (verse 22). Instead of killing Joseph, the brothers sell him into slavery. They lie to their father and say that Joseph was killed by a wild animal (verses 31-33).

Joseph ends up in Egypt and is bought by Potiphar who was the captain of the guard (chapter 39:1). Immediately Joseph is well favored and begins to prosper. Man can be sure that Satan has ways to disrupt any good that is happening. Joseph was in complete charge of Potiphar's house.

Joseph was a handsome young man and Potiphar's wife wanted him for herself. While her husband was away, she asked Joseph to "lie with her" (verse 7). Joseph refused because he knew it was wrong and he had too much respect for his master to commit such a sin. Most of all, he had respect for his great God! What an evil wife Potiphar had. She certainly did not have any of the virtues of the wife mentioned in Proverbs 31.

This story of Potiphar's wife shows how discreet men and women should be today. Thank God for wives and mothers who are faithful to their husbands and fathers. Joseph certainly is a role model for all today. Potiphar's wife lied about him and he was sent to prison, but God was with him (Genesis 39:14-21).

A Special Reward for Faithfulness

Even while he was in prison, Joseph used his time wisely. Joseph was elevated from prison to second in command in Egypt because he interpreted Pharaoh's dream. Genesis 41:16 tells why God blessed Joseph:

> And Joseph answered Pharaoh, saying, *It is* not in me:
> God shall give Pharaoh an answer of peace.

God is so mysterious and great. A seventeen-year-old youth was sold into slavery, resisted temptation, went to jail, interpreted a dream and saved a nation from starvation. Genesis 41:38-40 gives the story:

> And Pharaoh said unto his servants, Can we find such a one as this *is*, a man in whom the Spirit of God *is*? And Pharaoh said unto Joseph, Forasmuch as God hath shewed thee all this, *there* is none so discreet and wise as thou *art*: Thou shalt be over my house, and according unto thy word shall all my people be ruled: only in the throne will I be greater than thou.

After Joseph's exaltation, he takes a bride (notice that he takes a bride not brides). He and his wife, Asenath, were virgins when they married. God's desire is that the home be started with a husband and wife who have kept themselves sexually pure! Oh, how young people need to study the life of Joseph before they get married. The humanistic teachings of our day destroy the foundation of marriage and the home.

Joseph Saves Those Who Sought to Destroy Him

Joseph was not only a giant spiritually, but he was a giant mentally. He saw beyond the seven years of plenty and prepared for the seven years of famine. This is another lesson that the family needs to learn from Joseph. Too many live to the fullest in the good times and fail to prepare for the famine.

Someone said "You had better be careful whom you step on as you climb the ladder of success because you might need them on the way down." This was certainly true for Joseph's brothers. One can see the terrible famine described in Genesis 41 had reached Joseph's family, which was outside of Egypt. I had never heard the statement "Whatever goes around comes around" until I moved to North Augusta. What Joseph's brothers did to him came home quickly. Paul gives an excellent example in Galatians 6:7-8 when he says:

> Be not deceived; God is not mocked: for whatsoever a man soweth, that shall he also reap. For he that soweth to his flesh shall of the flesh reap corruption; but he that soweth to the Spirit shall of the Spirit reap life everlasting.

Jacob, even though his sons had lied to him about Joseph, kept the family together. He did what he could to provide for his family. When Jacob heard that there was corn in Egypt, he sent his sons to buy corn. Joseph knew his brothers but did not inform them who he was. Joseph tested them in prison for a short time. He let them return home with the understanding that they bring their younger brother back with them. Joseph kept Simeon as security. Genesis chapter 44 is a marvelous picture of sins coming home. In Genesis chapter 37, we see a group of hate-filled brothers willing to destroy their younger brother. They showed little respect and concern for their father as they lied to him about Joseph. Until Genesis chapter 44, they kept this lie from their father. In Genesis 44, they have been put to the test by Joseph. Joseph will keep Benjamin as a servant. The brothers are horrified. Why don't they lie again? Why are they so concerned about their younger brother and father now? Listen to Genesis 44:16:

> And Judah said, what shall we say unto my lord? What shall we speak? or how shall we clear ourselves? God hath found out the iniquity of thy servants behold, we are my lord's servants, both we, and *he* also with whom the cup is found.

Wouldn't it be great, if instead of going to the divorce court, or just walking out on our responsibilities, we would confess that all have failed and work together to solve the problems, whatever they might be? It is hard to imagine how this story might have ended had the brothers tried to lie their way out of Egypt.

How would you like to have been in the shoes of those brothers?

What a class act Joseph was! What a

model as a husband, father, brother and leader he was and is even for our day. Even though he is dead, he is a great model and example of righteousness for this day. He is an example of the grace and mercy of God. What a man of forgiveness he was. Listen to Genesis 45:4-6:

> And Joseph said unto his brethren, Come near to me I pray you. And they came near. And he said, I *am* Joseph your brother, whom ye sold into Egypt. Now therefore be not grieved, nor angry with yourselves, that ye sold me hither: for God did send me before you to preserve life. For these two years *hath* the famine *been* in the land: and yet, *there are* five years, in the which *there shall* neither *be* earing nor harvest.

How would you like to have been in the shoes of those brothers? My knees probably would have shaken worse than those of the western actor Fuzzie Q. Jones, who played in the movies with Randolph Scott. Fuzzie, when he got in a tough spot, could make his knees miss each other. But the marvelous thing about Joseph was his forgiving spirit. This kind of forgiveness would keep homes together today. Joseph saved his brothers and provided a good living place for Jacob and his family in Goshen.

Life certainly has its ups and downs.

From the first man and woman to the end of the life of Joseph, old Satan brought attack after attack upon the home. But through every situation, God's hand is seen. Consequently, those who obeyed the Lord and those who needed to be pruned, came forth victoriously. This is why, step by step, I believe God can have and give victory in the home today. It must be understood that victory only comes to those who are obedient to God's Word and way.

Moses Gives God's Guidelines for Life's Journey

Life certainly has its ups and downs. Just when Jacob and his family were enjoying their new found success, Egypt's leader died. The new king did not know Joseph and he put Israel in bondage. They were made to serve the people of Egypt. The king instructed the midwives to kill every Hebrew boy when they were born. The midwives feared the Lord and refused to kill the babies. Pharaoh later ordered that every boy born was to be drowned in the river.

Exodus chapter 2 gives a beautiful picture of God working in the lives of a family who seeks the best for their baby boy. It is exciting to see how God takes one family and uses them to impact the entire world.

When Moses was born, his mother and father hid him at home to keep the Egyptians from killing him. When they could hide him no longer, they prepared a basket and hid him in the river. God had his marvelous plan in order when the daughter of Pharaoh found Moses. This was no accident—it was the plan of God.

Moses is brought up in the home, educated in the land of the king who had demanded that the Hebrew boys be destroyed. Moses became the son of Pharaoh's daughter. Since he was brought up in the king's home, one would expect that Moses would take on the ways of the Egyptians, but his heart was with the Hebrew people. Listen to Hebrews 11:23-25:

> By faith Moses, when he was born, was hid three months of his parents, because they saw *he* was a proper child; and they were not afraid of the king's commandment. By faith Moses, when he was come to years, refused to be called the son of Pharaoh's daughter. Choosing rather to suffer affliction with the people of God, than to enjoy the pleasures of sin for a season.

In my opinion, there were two reasons why Moses made his decision to stay with his people. Number one is that God was in control and number two is that Moses had received his early training at the feet of his mother and father. A little sister also played an important part in the story. Moses' sister told Pharaoh's daughter where she could find a nurse for her brother. That nurse just

Every event was planned by God.

happened to be the mother of Moses. This event did not just happen. Every event was planned by God. Here again, God allows Moses to get the training that would help sustain him in the years ahead. No one can train a child as his own mother. It has always been and still is God's plan that a father and mother provide the training and leadership in the home.

When Moses fled for his life and left Egypt, he came to the land of Midian. It was here that Moses met his wife and started a family of his own (Exodus 2:21-22). Moses was content in Midian as he prospered and cared for his own family. But back in Egypt, God heard the cry of His children in bondage. Exodus 2:23-25 gives a vivid picture of what is happening:

> And it came to pass in process of time, that the King of Egypt died: And the children of Israel sighed by reason of the bondage, and they cried, and their cry came up unto God by reason of the bondage. And God heard their groaning, and God remembered his covenant with Abraham, with Isaac, and with Jacob. And God looked upon the children of Israel, and God had respect unto them.

When things are going so well, and we are minding our own business, God has his own way of interrupting things. Moses was surprised when he was confronted by God. Moses, without knowing it, had been preparing all of these years for what God had in store for him. You see, the little basket, the king's daughter, the little sister, the nurse, the home of the king, the Egyptian education and being driven to Midian were a part of God's sovereign design!

It did not take Moses a long time to find excuses for not returning to Egypt. Remember, he was wanted for murder back in Egypt. It seems that he had a pretty good excuse for not returning. But the command of God to return superceded his fear of returning. The person who had the murder warrant out in Egypt was dead by now. Listen to God's response to Moses' question in Exodus 3:13-14:

> And Moses said unto God, Behold, *when* I come unto the children of Israel, and shall say unto them, The God of your fathers hath sent me unto you; and they shall say to me, What is his name? what shall I say unto them? And God said unto Moses, I AM THAT I AM: and he said, thus shalt thou say unto the children of Israel, I AM hath sent me unto you.

Being persuaded by God, Moses begins his journey back to Egypt. Moses takes his wife and two sons with him. On the way, God "sought to kill him" (Exodus 4:24). Why would God seek to kill Moses, after he had commanded him to return to Egypt? According to The Pulpit Commentary, Moses had disobeyed God.[1] Back in Genesis 17:12, God had told Abraham that every male child "when he was eight days old must be circumcised." This was to be a sign of the covenant between man and God. It is doubtful that Moses had forgotten this command. Most likely, Zipporah his wife, was opposed to the ritual. Zipporah's actions recorded in Exodus 4:25-26 seems to support her opposition:

Obedience does not always demand that we like what God calls us to do.

> Then Zipporah took a sharp stone, and cut off the foreskin of her son, and cast *it* at his feet, and said, Surely a bloody husband *art* thou to me. So he let him go: then she said, A bloody husband *thou art*, because of the circumcision.

It certainly must have been difficult for Moses to prepare to lead the families of Israel when he was having family problems of his own. We do not know at what time, Moses sent his family back home but we do know when they returned (Exodus 18). It would be good to know that Zipporah supported Moses in his call when she came back, but we do not have that history. We do know from Exodus 4:25-26, that even though Zipporah did not agree with Moses about circumcision, she performed the act herself. Her decision saved Moses' life and protected God's covenant with his people. Obedience does not always demand that we like what God calls us to do. Practical thinking would lead us to believe that it is best for all concerned when one does agree with God's command.

We are thinking and decision making people.

In our homes today, there will be disagreements. Every husband and wife will have his or her differences. God did not make us robots. We are thinking and decision making beings. This sets us apart from the animals. Just because we do not agree, does not mean that we should become disagreeable and inflexible. When people become too stubborn to change, this does not mean to compromise with sin, little can be accomplished. But when a husband and wife can make decisions based on what is best for the family, God will bless that home. Selfishness is one of the main enemies and destroyers of the home.

What a Learning Experience From Egypt to the Promise Land

Before we become too critical of the Hebrew people and their journey, we had better take a good look at our own journey. Listen to what Peter says in I Peter 2:11:

> Dearly beloved, I beseech you as strangers and pilgrims, abstain from fleshly lusts, which war against the soul.

More attention will be given to our journey and how obedient we have been and are to the Bible in a later chapter.

After God's judgment culminated with the death of the first born in Egypt, the king urged Moses and his people to leave. The people of Egypt gave the Hebrew people all kinds of jewels, gold and silver to help them on their way. Exodus 12:37-38 gives some account of the number of people who left Egypt:

> And the children of Israel journeyed from Rameses to Succoth, about six hundred thousand on foot, *that were* men, beside children. And a mixed multitude went up also with them; and flocks, and herds, *even* very much cattle.

It is hard to imagine over a million people starting out on such a journey. Dr. Maclear in his Old Testament history states:

> The nearest route to Canaan would have been the usual caravan route, which runs in a northeasterly direction along the coast of the Mediterranean, and would not have occupied more than a few days.[2]

Exodus 13:17 points out that God chose another route because the people were not prepared to face the warlike Philistines. After God performed all of the miracles along the journey, it makes one wonder why God did not just "take the Philistines out of the way?" It is not always God's plan for us to know of the "whys". A study of the journey from Egypt to Canaan shows it was a tremendous learning experience for the Hebrews.

It is amazing how God works. He created man and woman who began the first home. When he had to judge the world because of wickedness, He found another man, Noah whom He could use to keep the home going. He spoke to Abraham and promised a son, Isaac, who would keep the home going. When Jacob and his family moved to Goshen, they were a small number. After 400 plus years of slavery and suffering, over a million people left the land of bondage and headed for the Promised Land. God's miracles continued as He protected the Hebrews with a pillar of clouds in the day, and a pillar of fire by night. He showed them His might and power by opening up the Red Sea in order that they might pass through on dry ground. The water stood up on either side as if it became a wall of ice. Some make fun of this story, but had they been there, they would have seen the miracle as it is described in the Bible! God makes the bitter water sweet, feeds them with manna and quails, gives water from the rocks and protects them from the enemy. What a mighty God the Hebrews had and He is just as mighty today. It is great to be excited about the God of miracles, but let's never lose sight of His grace and mercy. Even after each miracle, the crowd began to complain and murmur. Things have not changed in our day. God is so great, and yet, the majority is still living in disobedience. God could have left each family in the wilderness, but He had made a promise that some would enter the Promised Land!

Specific Guidelines for Family Living

How many blessings does unbelief rob us of today? What if the people had believed Caleb and Joshua rather than the ten who gave a false report about Canaan? We know that millions would have entered the Promised Land rather than dying in the wilderness. Through all of the trials in the wilderness, Moses, under God's directions, set up family structures and methods for worshipping the One True God. Exodus 20 gives the all-important account of the Ten Commandments.

Up to this time in history, we have little or no account of written instructions from God. But, listen to what Moses said in Deuteronomy 9:10:

> And the Lord delivered unto me two tables of stone written with the finger of God; and on them *was written* according to all the words, which the Lord spake with you in the mount out of the midst of the fire in the day of the assembly.

How important and marvelous are these commandments? The first four commandments deal with man's relationship and obedience to holy God. The fifth commandment shows the importance and respect God has for the home. The honor is for a "father and mother." Take that away and you pervert God's purpose for the home. As one looks at the last five commandments, it is easy to see the relationship to the family. This is how to respect and honor each other.

When God is first in a person's life, every thing else will fall into place. What a difference our world would be if every home had the respect and honor demanded in the commandments. Honor and respect should extend from one home to another. Just think what our world would be like if every person respected and honored what the other person had. It would be great if every neighbor was glad to see his neighbor prosper. If this were true, we would not have to worry about covetousness. There would be no stealing and killing. If every family respected each other's family, there would be no adultery. Adultery is the enemy of every home. In our day, instead of adultery being condemned, it is glorified. Just take a look at the magazines, movies and lifestyles and you will see the enemy everywhere. Just as we believe that there is One True God and that we should love our neighbor, there must be an understanding that God still means it when He says: "Thou shalt not commit adultery!" This commandment does not say it is all right in some circumstances but "thou shalt not." It seems very plainly to be saying, "no time at all."

Why Are People Afraid of the Ten Commandments?

Whether one does an in-depth study or just skims over the Ten Commandments, what he finds will be beneficial to him and those around him. Why, then, are school officials, legislators, the ACLU, and others so against the Ten Commandments being placed in public places? The debate over the separation of church and state, for many, is nothing more than a smoke screen to ban the name of Jesus Christ in public places. In my opinion, Madison and Jefferson, if they were alive today, would be ashamed of those who seek to keep the commandments out of public life.

Chapter V

You Cannot Disobey God's Law and Not Get Hurt

Just because a nation and culture sets up its own ideas of what is right or wrong, does not make it right in God's eyes. The Bible gives accounts of sinful actions in both the Old and New Testaments, but this does not mean that the Bible condones such actions. The Bible gives the story of Solomon and his many wives, but does not condone his actions. In fact, the Bible tells how his many wives turn him away from God. Hebrews chapter 7 gives a vivid picture of the torture of many saints, but certainly does not condone such torture.

As already stated in this study, it is the premise of this writer that God began the home with one man and one woman. This is clearly shown in Genesis 2:21-24. We are going to take a journey from Genesis through Malachi and see what happens when man tries to alter God's plan.

It is not known how many years have passed from Genesis 2 to Genesis 4. Skeptics and concerned alike have wondered where Cain got his wife. It must be remembered that people lived long lives in the beginning. It seems logical that Cain married his sister. By the time we read Genesis 4:19, there are distant cousins from which to chose a wife. Lamech was not satisfied with the one wife idea, so he chose two. We cannot blame this on pagan culture neither can we say that Lamech had a written command against having two wives. But the question must be asked, how much did Lamech know about Genesis 2:24? Granted nothing has been said about adultery until Exodus 20:14.

It is not known how much trouble Lamech had, if any, by having two wives. Yet, many have said, "no house is big enough for two families." They may, but it does not seem likely that two women could share the same man and same house without running into problems. It may have seemed <u>insignificant</u> at the <u>time</u>, but the shift from Genesis 2:24 (one woman) to Genesis 4:19 (two women) has brought pain and sorrow to many a home.

When a Person Runs Ahead of God, Look for Trouble

How can two people who have been so blessed of God get so far away from God? Abraham and Sarah both had experienced the mercy and grace of God. Yet, they decided to run ahead of God. Evidently, according to the law and culture of the day, it was all right for Abram to take Hagar as his wife and father a child by her. After all, it was Sarai's idea. Abram did not object and Hagar was just following orders like a good servant should. It is easy to find excuses and reasons for what was done. My, how things can get out of control. Look what happens as a result of Abram's and Hagar's relationship: (1) Sarai is despised in the eyes of Hagar; (2) Sarai blames Abram; (3) Sarai is jealous and is afraid that she will lose her husband and (4) Sarai wants God to judge between Sarai and Abram (Genesis 16:4-5). It is so easy to blame others when disobedience brings its fruits. In fact, some will even blame God!

We do not know how long Sarai had been planning this disobedience. She may have reasoned, "it is an accepted custom, so there is nothing wrong in giving Hagar to Abram." So, that which seemed accepted divided a home and has caused division between the Jews and Arabs down through history. What Abram and Sarai did years ago is affecting America economically, socially, spiritually and physically today. The tragedy of 9-11 saw hundreds of our people killed, our economy hurt, and neighbor turn against neighbor, and now, we are trying to rebuild Iraq. We are responsible for our actions today, but the seed of the problem can be traced back to the disobedience of Abraham and Sarah! There are those today who would laugh if they were told that the destroying of the Twin Towers in New York had its roots in Genesis 16:4. Hear the words today, "it was just an innocent look, it will not hurt anyone, they are having problems anyway and everyone is doing it." In a short period two homes are destroyed, a wife and husband are heartbroken and children are left without a father and mother to care for them! Abram should have known better, but that does not lessen the damage, it only adds to the guilt and blame.

Sin May be Committed in the Dark, but It Will Be Revealed in the Light

He was chosen king while he was still a lad, he killed a giant when he was just a youth, he walked with God in his times of trouble, but he fell at the height of his prosperity and glory. This man was David. The Bible says of him, "I have found a man after mine own heart (Acts 13:22)."

Any person who takes his eyes off Jesus is subject to fall.

David, of all people, had no excuse for the sins he committed. He was brought up in a good home. God allowed him to kill Goliath when the king and his army of Israel were deathly afraid of Goliath. God protected him when Saul sought to kill him. God gave him wisdom and wealth to lead his people. With all that David had going for him, how could he fall to such a low state? Sin is no respecter of persons. Any person, who takes his eyes off of Jesus, is subject to fall. Had David been on the battlefield rather than on the housetop, his life's story could have been much different.

How many times have you heard people say, "I never intended for this to happen"? II Samuel 11:1-17 gives a picture of how David sinned and how he tried to cover up his sin. The house where David lived was built so one could walk from the room to the housetop. The roof was flat so he could sit or walk around on the roof. While on the roof he saw a beautiful woman (Bathsheba) bathing. Being a man, he watched and was attracted by her beauty. But he watched too long! His gaze turned into lust. He sent for Bathsheba and she came to his house where they committed adultery. They both adulterated their marriage. One sin leads to another. They can no longer say, "We just had an affair while the husband was away." In their passion of sin, something happened which they never intended to happen. Bathsheba became pregnant. Sin has a way of coming home. Years ago, I heard a commencement speaker warn the young people when he said, "You can leave here tonight and play around, but in nine months the results of your playing around will come home!" What must David and Bathsheba do now? David is the king so he sent for Uriah, Bathsheba's husband. This would cover up the sin, so they thought! David sent Uriah home, but Uriah slept at the king's door. He would not go in and enjoy a time with his wife while his men were on the battlefield. What an honorable soldier and man Uriah was. Since David's plan backfired, David ordered that Uriah be put on the front line of battle so he would be killed. Sin is so deceptive and cruel. David then took Bathsheba as his wife. By this time, David had multiplied his sin.

David Receives a Visit From the Preacher

Uriah is dead, Bathsheba is over here crying, and David has another wife. The sin has been covered up, so all is well. But according to II Samuel 11:27, "this displeased the Lord." Oh, if people today would realize that they cannot hide sin.

Nathan, the prophet of God, confronted David about his great sin. David confessed that he had sinned. After his confession, David received these words: (1) you shall not die, (2) what you have done caused the enemies to blaspheme God and (3) the child shall die (II Samuel 12:13-14).

People love to say, "but God will forgive any sin." We should thank God that he does. But too many times, these same people fail to realize the consequences and scars sins bring, even though they have been forgiven. Psalms 51 is a beautiful example of God's forgiveness and restoration. But, let the passage show the repentance and confession of David, and the changes in his life.

I would be amiss if I failed to show how David's life was scarred by his sin. II Samuel 12:33 tells that the child died and II Samuel 13 tells the story of how Amnon rapes Tamar and shames her. These are David's children by different wives. II Samuel also tells how Absalom, the brother of Tamar, kills Amnon and all of his brothers. Absalom turned against his own father and tried to steal the kingdom from him. Finally, listen to the agony of David in II Samuel 18:33:

> And the king was much moved, and went up to the chamber over the gate and wept: and as he went, thus he said, O my son Absalom, my son, my son Absalom! Would God I had died for thee, O Absalom, my son, my son!

Although David had been forgiven for his transgressions, one must wonder how many times, he must have said, "If I had not been on the housetop and if I had not sent for Bathsheba." This is not to say that all people who have trouble are being punished for sin. Some of the godliest people in the world seem to have the most trouble. Paul is a good example (Romans 8:35-39). The things which happened to David and his family, seem to point back to his sin. In fact, Psalms 51:3 says, "For I acknowledge my transgressions: and my sin is ever before me."

David's sin and the results point out that sin will "find us out" (Numbers 32:23). Yet, through all that David endured, he experienced the grace and forgiveness of God. Husbands, wives and children can learn from the experiences in the life of David. Had David been on the battlefield rather than on the housetop, his home life would, no doubt, have been quite different. If today's homes would follow the advice given in Ephesians 6:10-17, things would be much different. We would have solid homes rather than broken homes.

Forgiveness Is the Glue That Keeps a Family Together

If you want to study a beautiful picture of romance, read the Song of Solomon. But, if you want to see a marriage saved when sin had entered, read carefully the book of Hosea.

It is amazing how many churches and pastors look for ways to justify divorce and remarriage. George Barna, in his survey of broken marriages, points out that so called evangelical Christians are more likely to divorce and remarry than those who are atheistic or agnostic.[1]

God uses the story of Hosea and Gomer to show His loving concern for Israel. Hosea preached during the time of Amos, Isaiah and Micah. Gomer lived among a very sinful people. Her story and that of Hosea shows that no matter how far or low a person is in sin, God still loves and wants to forgive. Hosea 1:2 says, "…take unto thee a wife of whoredoms and children of whoredoms…." This is a difficult passage and seems to be saying that Gomer is already an impure young woman. But, when the complete chapter is read, it appears that Gomer was a pure woman who lived in a very sinful time among very sinful people. By the time Gomer had her fourth child, she had already become an unfaithful wife. This child did not belong to Hosea. Gomer had become an adulterous wife. God pictured Himself as the husband of Israel who had also become adulterous. Scofield says, "Israel Jehovah's adulterous wife repudiated, but ultimately to be purified and restored."[2]

Gomer turned her back on her family and lived the life of a fallen woman (harlot). If any one had a right to get rid of a wife, Hosea did. But you see, he loved her. His love was more than physical (Epithumia), romance (Eros), natural affection (storge), friendship (phileo) but rather it was unconditional love (agape). Although Gomer had gone to the bottom, Hosea bought her back. He took her home, set her apart and took her back again for himself and no other. You talk about love and you can see it in the life of this man and woman. Some will ask, "How could he take her back after she had lived such a sinful life?" It is not a matter of "how could he," but rather that he did. Every pastor and every judge when asked to be part of a broken marriage should require those involved to read the book of Hosea. It may be helpful for the preacher and the judges to read Hosea also. It could bring a halt to many broken marriages.

Hosea paid for a wife who already belonged to him. Israel belonged to God by creation and calling, but she forsook Him for other gods. Yet in the midst of all her sins, He promised restoration and forgiveness. Finally God sent His blessed son, who also bought us back. Listen to I Peter 1:18-19:

> Forasmuch as ye know that ye were not redeemed with corruptible things, as silver and gold, from your vain conversation received by tradition from your fathers; but with the precious blood of Christ, as a lamb without blemish and without spot.

Hosea paid for a wife who already belonged to him.

Just as Israel was portrayed as the wife of God in the Old Testament, the church is portrayed as the bride of Christ today. God loved Israel and even though He had to punish her for her sins, He offered forgiveness.

The church, at times, doesn't look much like a bride, but she is being prepared for a great wedding. Even when the church sins, there is forgiveness when there is true repentance. Hosea did not let his wife, Gomer, stay in the slave market. Jesus will not allow the church, His bride, to stay in the slave market of sin.

What a turn around for the home, if like Hosea, there was forgiveness and restoration rather than separation. But when trouble comes to the home today very little is said about Hosea. It is easy and natural for the lost person to say, "I just cannot forgive because of what he or she has done." But for the Christian, he is not dealing with the natural, but rather with the supernatural. The Christian knows what it means to be forgiven. No one deserves the forgiveness of Christ, but even while we were in sin, He died for us (Romans 5:8).

It would be heart rending to know how many wives and husbands said to their mate, in the last week, "I don't want to be married anymore." Many times the ones making such statements don't stop to realize the hurt, embarrassment and shame they bring to those around them. Many godly wives, who love and care for their families are just devastated when they find out that their husband has been unfaithful. Hard working men are left to answer the question, "What went wrong?" when a wife leaves for someone else. The real tragedy is when children are involved. Children are so confused when they have "part-time parents."

Broken homes bring pain and separation in our churches. As a pastor, I have witnessed the rumors, finger pointing and finally the separation as the truth surfaced about affairs between members. Many times, when the truth comes to the light, members are horrified to find out who are involved. Along with the hurt and disappointment, anger sets in. Not only are homes destroyed but scars are placed upon the church and her testimony.

The statistics are alarming when you read or hear, "pastor or staff runs off with the church secretary or musician or some woman in the church." Such affairs take years, if ever, for such stigmas to be removed from those churches. It is easy to say, "They just got caught in a bad situation or pastors and staff are human, too." As Henry Brandt says in his book, The Heart of the Matter, "Sin is the Problem." Just think of the people who are hurt. When leaders, who are so visible, go astray, look what it does to the trust factor. Some will even say, "I will never trust any pastor or staff member any more!" When Jim Baker and Jimmy Swaggart fell, I over heard a woman say, "I don't trust any preacher any more." That statement angered me because I knew she was being unfair. My anger and knowing that she was being unfair did not change how she felt about preachers. Thank God for His forgiveness and mercy when those who fall truly repent! But, we must remember that repentance and forgiveness do not remove the scars and hurt brought by sin.

Forty to fifty percent of the leadership in many churches are divorced and remarried. This is not to say that God is not using those in such places. God does forgive when there is repentance. If God is using those leaders now, just think how much more He could have used them had they not broken his command in the beginning.

Some churches have pastors and deacons who are divorced and remarried. If one does an honest and careful study of the qualifications both in Titus and Timothy, he will realize that divorce and remarriage disqualifies a person from being a pastor or deacon.

If Abraham were alive today, would he run ahead of God and father a child by Hagar? I think not! If he could see the fighting and killing between the Arabs and Jews, he would say, "the price is too great!"

Ask David, "Knowing the consequences would you still have Bathsheba come to your house?" "NO-NO, the price is too great." "Look at what happened to my family and what it cost me as a father, husband and king."

The examples given in this study from the Old Testament will be helpful to the homes and families if studied carefully. Malachi, the last writer in the Old Testament, has some sobering statements about divorce and remarriage. He says in Malachi 2:11-12 and 16:

> Judah hath dealt treacherously, and an abomination is committed in Israel and in Jerusalem; for Judah hath profaned the holiness of the Lord which he loved, and hath married the daughter of a strange god. The Lord will cut off the man that doeth this, the master and the scholar, out of the tabernacles of Jacob, and him that offereth an offering unto the Lord of hosts. For the Lord, the God of Israel saith that he hateth putting away (divorce).

The men of Malachi's day were divorcing their wives and remarrying younger, pagan wives. Moses, in the beginning, warned his people against marrying pagan wives. These men paid no attention to the law. They put their legitimate wives away and committed adultery. These men thought they could sin and still worship and sacrifice to Holy God. They came to the worship center while their "put away wives" cried at the altar.

What a picture of our day. Many will have an affair, put their wife or husband away by divorce, and come to the church for forgiveness. God does forgive any sin you know. People today are knowingly committing sin while saying, "I will ask for forgiveness later." Where is the repentance? Man's ideas today are just as treacherous and abominable as they were in Malachi's day!

It is heartbreaking to look on the face of a young man and see the agony after his wife has just said, "I don't love you anymore, I have found someone else." What a shame, when little children look up at their mother and ask, "When is daddy coming home?" God, if there is true repentance, will forgive those who cause such hurt, but things will never be the same again. The damage has been done and the scars will remain. But what is so sinful and arrogant are those who have caused such pain, yet still expect to worship God without any notion of repentance and restoration. Many expect to be leaders in the church and will dare any preacher to call their hand. If we had more Nathans today, we would have more Davids who cry out for forgiveness and cleansing.

Chapter VI

God Solidified the Foundation of the Home By Sending His Blessed Son

During this Christmas season, my mind goes back to the beautiful words of Micah in chapter 5:2 when he said:

> But thou, Bethlehem Ephratah, *though* thou be little among the thousands of Judah, *yet* out of thee shall he come forth unto me *that* is to be ruler in Israel; whose goings forth *have been* from of old, from everlasting.

It is amazing to realize that God sent His blessed son to be a part of a family and home. Philippians 2:6-8 gives a beautiful picture of how the Lord Jesus identified Himself with mankind.

God Sends Mary a Startling Message

We do not know how long Mary had been engaged to Joseph. It can be surmised that Joseph and Mary were looking forward to their pending wedding with excitement and joy. Since this Jewish couple was engaged, there were no known reasons why they should not be married. In fact, this engagement could only be broken by divorce. Mary receives the shock of her life when God sends her a message by the angel Gabriel (Luke 1:26-38). Mary no doubt was surprised and excited that God would pay attention to her (verse 28). Mary's anxiety turned to fear when the angel told her that she would have a son (verse 31). This was not to be any ordinary son, but the Son of God (verse 32-33). Mary knew this could not be, because she had never "known" a man (verse 34). When Mary said, "I know not a man" (verse 34) she was simply saying that she was

No one but Joseph and the Lord could understand Joseph's hurt when he found out that Mary was pregnant.

a pure woman and had saved herself for her to be husband, Joseph. When Gabriel explained God's plan to her, she surrendered to God's plan (verse 38). Even though Mary surrendered to God's plan, how would Joseph accept this news? When things seem to be most difficult, God is able to supply our every need (Philippians 4:19). During the stormy times, God can calm the billows (Philippians 4:6-7).

In the Midst of Hurt and Confusion, Joseph Learns Obedience

No one but Joseph and the Lord could understand Joseph's hurt when he found out that Mary was pregnant. His world came crashing down as his dreams of a marriage to Mary were crushed! How could it be that Mary, whom he thought was so pure, could deceive him? Who was the person she had had an affair with while saying she wanted to be his bride? Even though Joseph was angry and hurt, he still loved Mary. According to the law, Mary could be brought before the public and stoned. Joseph did not want her shamed and stoned (Matthew 1:19). God had other plans! When the angel of the Lord explained God's plan to Joseph, he obediently took Mary as his wife (Matthew 1:18-25).

During the months ahead, Joseph and Mary would endure harsh looks and quiet whispers as the crowds passed by. Some probably called Joseph foolish for marrying a "fallen woman." If the crowd only knew that Mary was carrying the Son of God, things would be different. There are still those who deny the virgin birth today. According to the crowd, "It was impossible for God to have become man." Yet, that is exactly what happened (Philippians 2:5-11). People were blinded in Joseph and Mary's day, and many are still blind today (I Corinthians 2:14).

What a joy it is for a young couple when their first child is born. There are the best doctors and best facilities to welcome the birth of the new one. When the baby is born, he receives the best care and everything is done for his or her protection.

What a difference that night when Jesus was born. There were no doctors or facilities if something had gone wrong. His crib and clothing were those of the poorest family. But out on the mountainside His birth was announced by the angels of heaven. God's glory lit up the sky. An announcement was made that would affect the whole world; God's Son of redemption had come (Luke 2:11).

Before and after the birth of Jesus, Mary and Joseph's home life was probably one of wonder and expectation. An example of this is when the wise men visited and worshipped Jesus in the home (Matthew 2:11-12). When Joseph was directed by an angel to flee to Egypt to escape with Jesus from Herod, you see the tender love of a father and husband (Matthew 2:13-15).

For some reason, very little is said in the scriptures about the early childhood and youth years of Jesus. Luke lets us know that he "grew in wisdom and spirit, and the grace of God was upon him" (Luke 2:40). Luke also gives the amazing account of Jesus when at twelve years of age He confounded the religious leaders. When his parents found him, he said to them:

> How is it that ye sought me? wist ye not that I must be about my Father's business? (Luke 2:49)

Since we know very little about the early years of Jesus, it is left to our imagination as to what kind of home life He had. Jesus probably had a normal home life like most of the youngsters of His day. Fables have been written about Him using magical powers, but we can be assured that He would not have done anything which would not have glorified His heavenly father! Joseph and Mary were probably normal parents who taught Jesus along with the rest of the family the ways of God.

Jesus Provides the Example for the Home and the Church

After Jesus was baptized, He was led into the wilderness and was tempted by Satan. Even though He was God, He was also man and overcame the temptations of Satan. Sometime later, He made this marvelous declaration:

> The Spirit of the Lord is upon me, because he hath anointed me to preach the gospel to the poor; he hath sent me to heal the brokenhearted, to preach deliverance to the captives, and recovering of sight to the blind, to set at liberty them that are bruised. To preach the acceptable year of the Lord. (Luke 4:18-19)

This passage shows how Jesus will guide the home and church to victory when people will allow Him. When the home or the church is destroyed, it is because individuals refuse to follow the guidelines left by Jesus. According to Hebrews 4:15, Jesus has faced and won the victory over every temptation that man will ever face. He also promised "mercy" and grace in the time of need (Hebrews 4:16).

When one listens to the radio, watches TV, or reads the newspaper, he is perplexed by what is happening to the home. The divorce rate is sky high. More people are living together rather than marrying, and what some call an "alternate lifestyle" is gaining support. Is there any wonder that homes are on the rocks and many children are in rebellion? But what can one expect when the Bible is ridiculed and it is against the law to pray and mention the name of Jesus in public places? When man puts his standards above God's standards, disaster is the result!

Listen to some biblical standards for a home. The Lord must be the builder if a home is to last (Psalms 127:1). This makes sense if God is our creator and also established the home, it's not only reasonable to let Him be in charge; it is a must!

Nina and I have been married over fifty years and how I praise God that He is our guide and fortress. It has not always been easy, but God has always been faithful. When we first married, we rented a little two-room house. We sealed the living room ceiling with cardboard. Yet, we were happy because Jesus was and is our Lord. Today, over fifty years later we have three grown sons, six grandchildren, one great-grandchild, and a gorgeous home. During these years, there have been valleys and mountains, but God has been our guide. Jesus gave the perfect example of how a home can stand the test of time when He said:

> Therefore whosoever heareth these sayings of mine, and doeth them, I will liken him unto a wise man which built his house upon a rock: And the rain descended, and the floods came, and the winds blew, and beat upon that house; and it fell not: for it was founded upon a rock. (Matthew 7:24-25)

If people would only take God at His word, they would not be destroyed by the storms of life. Storms do and will come! But if the foundation is on Christ, the storms will leave their marks, but the foundation will stand secure!

If the home is to survive, Christians must marry Christians. It is essential for two people who commit themselves in marriage to have the same values and ideals. The words of Amos could apply to marriage when he said: "can two walk together, except they be agreed?" (Amos 3:3). A Christian who is about to marry a non-Christian should heed Paul's warning in II Corinthians 6:14. He should especially listen to the warnings of Jesus when He said:

> And every one that heareth these sayings of mine, and doeth them not, shall be likened unto a foolish man which built his house upon the sand: And the rain descended, and the floods came, and the winds blew, and beat upon that house; and it fell: and great was the fall of it. (Matthew 7:26-27)

Jesus, by His actions, showed His love for the home and family. The first miracle of our Lord was at a wedding in a home (John 2:11). Jesus showed His love and compassion for a woman who came from a broken home (John 4:17-18). Jesus showed his love for families when He fed them (John 6:11). Jesus healed the maniac of Gadara and told him to "go home to his family" (Mark 5:19). Jesus gave the story of the wayward sons (Luke 15:11-32). Jesus showed His love for and the importance of children (Luke 18:17). Jesus had fellowship in the home of Martha and Mary (Luke 10:38-39). At the cross, while He was dying,

Jesus provided for His mother (John 19:26-27). These events are not necessarily in chronological order, but they show the concern of Jesus for the family and the home.

Chapter VII

What Are Some Historical Events Which Have Helped Weaken the Foundation of the Home?

Up to this point in the study of the home, the information and remarks have been related to the Old Testament and the early years of the New Testament. The scene now shifts to the discovery of America and what part the home played in her history. Many things, good and bad, can happen in 515 years. That is from 1492 to 2007. America has been a free nation, 1776 to 2007, for 231 years.

Why Did People Come to America?

When one studies history, he will find that people came to America for different reasons. Some, like those from Spain, came for gold and religious reasons. A study of South America will reveal that the Catholic religion was established, but a look at the churches with all of the gold inside shows how much wealth was taken from the land. Many came from England looking for religious and political freedom. Many came looking for a place where they could work and take care of their families.

From Jamestown to Plymouth Rock, the "new found territory" was ablaze with courage, suffering and death!

In order to see what events in American history have weakened the foundation of the home, an honest look must be given to those events which provided a solid foundation for the home in the beginning. From Jamestown to Plymouth Rock, the "new found territory" was ablaze with courage, suffering, and death. Immediately someone will ask, "What has this to do with the family?" When you look at the thirteen original colonies, from Massachusetts to Georgia, families struggled to survive. There could be no government, schools, or churches without the home.

When I visited the Indian fort in Boonesboro, Kentucky some years ago, I could not help but think of the courage and determination of those early settlers as they fought off the Indians. In my home, I can enjoy my grandchildren because of the courage of those before me! Because Daniel Boone fought for his family and those around him, this could be said of him in his latter years:

> Surrounded by his children, his grandchildren and his great-grandchildren, he spun tales of his exploits in Kentucky, of his adventures while hunting and of living among the Indians. It is said that when one of his children asked him if he had ever been lost, he replied, "Can't say I was ever lost, but there were times when I was plum confused.[1]

It is one thing to read about the Alamo or watch the story on television, but it is something else to stand on the spot where those brave people died in 1836. The courage of such a small group against such overwhelming odds shows how the home and family have survived through the years. The following is said about the western frontier:

> Western frontier life in America marks one of the most exciting chapters in American history. This settlement of the west represented the dreams of gold hungry prospectors and of homesteaders whose backbreaking labor transformed barren plains into fields of grain. It is the story of cowboys and the open Range. It is the drama of Indians and outlaws of trains and stage coaches they attacked, and citizens who brought order to the frontier. It is a living tradition that symbolizes to men and women everywhere the American achievement of taming a wild and beautiful land.[2]

From Valley Forge, to the signing of the Declaration of Independence and the Constitution of the United States, we see the importance of the family. Those men with General George Washington at Valley Forge had left their families to fight for freedom. The men who signed the Declaration of Independence risked their lives and those of their families in order that the home could be free. As one studies the Constitution of the United States of America with all of its protection of rights for the individual, he must realize that if the home is destroyed, there will be no individual to enjoy these protected rights!

The Civil War marks one of the saddest times in American history. More men were killed in this war than all of the previous wars or those which have followed. Whichever side one may take as to who was right, it must be agreed that both sides were willing to die for what they believed. It was so sad for brother to fight against brother and family against family.

In fact, the conditions of some whites were as poor as those of the blacks.

Before the south and north went to war in the 1860s, the south relied on farming, while the north relied on farming, trading, and shipping. Much of the work in the north was done by free labor, while the south used slave labor.[3]

After the Civil War, the north became a more industrial region, while the south continued farming. The south suffered greatly during the reconstruction. Much has been said and written about the plight of the Negroes in the south, but until the early 1950s, it was not unnatural to see blacks and whites working in the fields together. In fact, the conditions of some whites were as poor as those of the blacks. The point being, no matter the race, the family was close and very important.

The World Wars I and II, Korea, Vietnam, Persian Gulf, and now Iraq have had tremendous effects upon family values, both economically and socially. These effects will be discussed in the next section.

It Is so Easy to Forget How We Got Where We Are

The secular humanist will deny that America was established, mostly, by those who believed in the Judeo-Christian faith. However, a reading of the Mayflower Compact (1620) where it says: "Having undertaken, for the glory of God and advancement of the Christian faith"[4] certainly disagrees with the humanist. In my opinion, those who use this idea of "Separation of Church and state" as a means to protect any religion, miss what the signers of the Bill of Rights really meant. It certainly does not mean an "absence of God." And yet, there are those who want to do away with the mention of God, and especially the name of Jesus! A careful study of history will show that John Lealand, a devout Baptist influenced James Madison in the wording of the first Amendment to the Constitution. Certainly, it would be unfair to put words in Mr. Madison's mouth, but one must wonder if his ideas about "Separation of Church and State" would be near those of the Baptist Joint commission or the ACLU? I doubt that Mr. Madison would have been opposed to Bible reading and prayer in schools.

Education in the colonies was provided by the churches in order that the people could read the Bible for themselves. Harvard was founded in 1636 and Yale in 1701. Both of these colleges were established as Christian schools.

As the United States grew, elementary and high schools were established. During the early years, mostly those who came from wealthy families were able to attend school. As has been stated earlier, farming both in the north, but especially in the south, was the primary means of making a living. Due to this, most family members had to work on the farm. This being the case, many received little or no education.[5]

The end of World War II brought a drastic change to the culture and morals of America. Segregation in the military had been outlawed. The men and women who had served so bravely came home with the idea of receiving all the rights and benefits due to every citizen no matter the color of ones skin. But it was also during this time that the divorce rate began to climb. Many families were fractured. As a result of the war, many women went to work in the defense plants. This gave women a new freedom, but it also provided a problem for the home and the children. Grandparents and daycare centers can provide much needed help, but no one can take the place of a mother. Merle Burke in his History of the United States says:

> The absence of working together as a unit for a common cause has undoubtedly aided our rising divorce rate and has contributed considerably to the increase in the number of broken homes. And always, when a home is divided, it's the children who suffer.[6]

The Brown verses Board of Education (1954) Act, which ended segregation, or at least, was the beginning of the end, brought good and different problems for the races. For the Negroes, the decision brought new freedoms, which were too long in coming. In the case of the whites, changes began to take place socially, psychologically, and spiritually. This did not mean that utopia had arrived, but it did mean that black and white families related to each other much better than in the past.

Two political decisions, one in 1962 and one in 1963, drastically affected the home, school, and churches. In 1962, the Supreme Court ruled that there could be no state supported prayer in schools.[7] The key, in my opinion, is "state supported." Today, in most schools, there is no prayer in the classroom and students are not allowed to have a blessing at mealtime. It is my opinion that the Supreme Court never intended such strict opposition to prayer. It seems that school and political officials have reacted out of fear of the ACLU and liberal groups.

In 1963 Madalyn Murray O'Hair, an atheist brought a suit against Bible reading in the schools. The Supreme Court ruled that there could be no required Bible reading in the schools.[8] Again, in my opinion, the term "required" is the key. Just as in the case of prayer, it seems that officials have reacted out of fear of lawsuits by the ACLU and other liberal and humanistic groups. Regardless of the reason, when prayer and Bible reading were removed, an erosion of values and morals began which continues to this day.

When I was in public school (1940-50), it was a joy to begin class with prayer and Bible reading and the Pledge to the flag. Values and morals taught at home were continued in school. Discipline at home would be continued at school. Right from wrong and black and white, which were taught at home, were continued in school. Today, in most schools, discipline is a thing of the past. There was a time when students respected their teachers and were respectful in all areas. In this day of enlightenment, teachers cannot instruct in the areas of right and wrong or moral values. Things are no longer black and white, but rather shades of gray. Absolutes are out dated and tolerance is the word of the day. Years ago, parents did not have to be worried about improper materials being taught to their children, but that is no longer true. Some educators and those who write school materials, because of their own beliefs and pressure from liberal groups, are pushing materials which advocate alternate life styles (homosexuality) and a new age ideology.

When I taught school (1965-68), it was a pleasure to see students learn and grow. This is a far cry from today. When there were discipline problems, I handled them myself. In fact, my students made me a paddle and named it "Old Betsy." Did I use it? You bet I did! Certainly caution was used and I had order in my class. One teacher said the other day that a student said "get out of my face" to her when she attempted to correct her. Thank God for good administrators and good teachers. I could not teach today because if a student got in my face or talked back to me, I would get fired or put in prison! It is no wonder that many schools have become battlegrounds. You know, when schools had prayer and Bible reading and discipline and value-morals were taught, we did not have all these problems.

When God is not honored in the home, problems begin to arise in the churches, schools, and states. Much of the rebellion today, whether social, political, psychological, or religious can be traced to the hippie movement of the 60's and 70's. This group not only protested against the war in Vietnam, but against the values of the home, church and society. While protesting the war, they lived together, drank, did drugs, and partied together. They came up with their own ideas of love, sex, and lifestyle.[9] While they protested against the war as being unjust, they did not seem to think about the sinfulness of their own lifestyle and the consequences of such. Even today, while our young men and women are fighting to liberate the people of Iraq, people are protesting around the world. In some parts of the world, they protest against the war, yet cry "kill Americans." Those who protest in America against the war and killing will march for the rights of a woman to kill her unborn baby! When we see how mixed up and confused many parents are, is it any wonder that our youth are so confused? Jesus said, "Can the blind lead the blind? Shall they not both fall into the ditch?" (Luke 6:39).

When God's Blueprint Is Ignored, Expect Faulty Results

God's message to the children of Israel in Deuteronomy 8:11-20 is so appropriate for America today. What a warning to the family this is. God provided every opportunity for His chosen people to live in plenty in their fine homes. But He reminded them that in order for their homes to be blessed, they must be obedient to Him. If they chose not to be obedient, He would destroy them just as He did their enemies before them! God has a special blessing for the home that is obedient to Him (Proverbs 12:7). The survival of any nation depends upon the homes obedience to sovereign God (Psalms 127:1).

We sing proudly "God Bless America" and He surely has! I can just imagine that those early settlers at Jamestown called upon God. A reading of the Mayflower Compact, leads us to believe that those early pilgrims had their trust in Holy God. Thanksgiving Day, for us, is a reminder of that first Thanksgiving when the pilgrims invited the Indians to a meal as they thanked God for His "provisions".

In the early days of the North American colonies, Christianity played a vital role in the home. But by the early 1700's, the religious fires began to dim. The following statement was made:

> The colonies needed a spiritual awakening. In New England the Half-Way Covenant was slowly filling the Congregationalist's churches with unconverted members. Some areas, such as the frontier regions of the Carolinas, had almost no religious life of any kind. Many attended church out of tradition. There was no guarantee that even ministers were converted.[10]

The period of the Great Awakening lasted about 40 years. There are those who say the Great Awakening lasted from 1740-1742, but its effects lasted much longer. When you study the lives of men like Jonathan Edwards, George Whitefield, Samuel Davis, Daniel Marchall and Shubal Stearns, you can see the impact that the Great Awakening had on the colonies. The lives and teachings of these men, no doubt, had a profound effect on the home life of the day.

Why is it that when the thirteen colonies became the United States of America that she had such a solid principle in her Constitution, laws, Biblical principles, and values? In this writer's opinion, it is because the leaders of this great country, in the beginning, were taught their values in the home. Listen to what President George Washington said:

> Whereas it is the duty of all nations to acknowledge the providence of Almighty God, to obey His will, to be grateful for His benefits, and humbly to implore His protection and favor.[11]

But listen to the liberals today as they argue that we are a "diverse people" and there are many gods. I am glad that President Washington prayed to "Almighty God" and not many gods. I am so thankful that our current President, George Bush, is not ashamed to acknowledge his faith in God and His Son, Jesus Christ.

Before he became president, John Adams wrote in his diary dated February 22, 1756, these words:

> Suppose a nation in some distant region should take the Bible for their only law book, and every member should regulate his conduct by the precepts there exhibited! Every member would be obliged in conscience, to temperance, frugality, and industry; to justice, kindness, and charity towards his fellow men; and to piety, love, and reverence toward Almighty God…What a Utopia, what a Paradise would this region be.[12]

Wow! What a statement about the Bible. Where have all the great leaders gone? Sir William Blackstone who played a leading role in forming the basis of law in America said:

> The doctrines thus delivered we call the revealed or divine law, and they are to be found only in Holy Scriptures... [and] are found upon comparison to be really part of the original law of nature. Upon these two foundations, the law of nature and the law of revelation, depend all human laws; that is to say, no human laws should be suffered to contradict these.[13]

Evidently, the United States Supreme Court members did not study Sir Blackstone's works when Bible reading and prayer were ruled out of our schools and they approved the right to kill babies. The Ninth Circuit State Supreme Court must have had their eyes and ears closed when they ruled it is unconstitutional to say "under God" in the Pledge of Allegiance. God, please give us men and women of integrity. It is no wonder that the foundations of homes are being eroded while we have such leadership in our country. The words of Thomas Jefferson, excerpts of which are engraved on the Jefferson Memorial in Washington, D.C. should be heeded by Americans today:

> God who gave us life gave us liberty. Can the liberties of a nation be secure when we have removed a conviction that these liberties are the gift of God? Indeed I tremble for my country when I reflect that God is just, that His justice cannot sleep forever.[14]

It seems, that is to me, that the ACLU, The Baptist Joint Commission, and other liberals have only read part of what Thomas Jefferson said and wrote when they use his sayings to prove their way of removing God from society.

It is not hard to believe that George Washington, John Adams, Thomas Jefferson, James Madison along with Jonathan Edwards, John

Lealand and with many other political, as well as Christian, leaders fought for the purity of the home, church, and nation. It is so tragic to see the foundations of the home, church, and nation being destroyed. Much is being said about "my rights" and "my liberty". But if rights and liberty are gifts from God, what will happen if God is removed from society? The very thing that people call freedom is nothing more than Anarchy!

Has Christian Education Failed the Home?

"What a ridiculous question," some will say. But it is a question which we must honestly research and then draw our conclusions. It is one thing to say a school is Christian but being Christian is quite different.

Harvard was established as a Christian school, but like many others after her, she drifted into liberalism. Dr. Crawford H. Toy, a brilliant teacher at Southern Baptist Seminary, resigned in 1879 to become a professor at Harvard. In the beginning, Dr. Toy was a staunch supporter of the total truthfulness of scripture. But as he began to do further study in higher criticism, he rejected the total truthfulness of scripture. His views then and now appeal to the liberal mind and those who reject Biblical inerrancy. In fact, until lately his views were widely held and taught in many of our Southern Baptist Seminaries. As students received such teachings and returned to our churches and presented such, is it any wonder that there is such confusion in our homes and churches. The following will give a better understanding of who Dr. Toy was:

> Through the years, there has been an unusual interest in the Toy case. John R. Sampey, the professor of Old Testament interpretation at Southern Seminary in the early twentieth century,has been reported as saying that Broadus had noticed "marked Unitarians tendencies in (Toy's) thinking" and that this supposed Unitarianism was the real reason his resignation was accepted. Irwin T. Hyatt, Jr., reports that Toy did in fact join the Unitarian

> Church when he went to Harvard to become Hancock professor of Hebrew and other Oriental Languages.[15]

Just think how many of our young people are taught in our so called prestigious colleges and universities. If the theology and religious departments are liberal, what does that say for the social, political, and psychological departments? Just the other day a young student, whose father is in Iraq, stated that a professor in his school said "the American soldiers should be shot." Can you imagine such a statement being said in one of our leading universities by a professor? This professor, in my opinion, is un-American and a traitor. He should have been fired on the spot. But no, the elite and intellectuals say this is "academic freedom." This came right after another professor in Florida had been relieved of his duty when it was alleged that he was supporting terrorists. The educational system in American colleges, universities, seminaries, high schools, and elementary schools needs to get back to the values and guidelines of the Bible. It is tragic that many young people become confused when they are faced with a professor who rejects all of the values and teachings of the home and church. An ungodly professor or teacher can be more dangerous than a terrorist. We send our young men to foreign countries to liberate others while allowing teachings and practices in our own country which will, if allowed to continue, destroy our homes, churches, and nation.

An ungodly professor or teacher can be more dangerous than a terrorist.

Some years ago, when the Southern Baptist Convention met in Orlando, Florida, Josh McDowell warned the messengers how the word tolerance would be changed and used in the years ahead. Boy, was he right. Tolerance is a noun, which means I recognize your right to believe as you do even though I don't agree with your belief. Tolerant is an adjective and means that what you believe really does not bother me. Tolerate is a verb and means that I will not do anything to hinder another person's belief.[16]

What the humanist wants, since there is no god, according to them, is for everyone to accept each other's beliefs as being equal. What has happened, as a result of such reasoning, is that the Christian home and church have bought into this lie! When a person does take a stand against evil, politically or socially he is branded as a bigot!

Southern Baptists have been blessed with great educators such as Dr. Broadus, A. T. Roberson, B. H. Carroll, and many others. We have had great preachers who have stood for the truth such as George Truett, R. G. Lee, W. A. Criswell, and many, many more. These teachers and pastors stood against modernism and those things which were a danger to the home, church, and nation.

But in a subtle way, when our educators received their training in European universities where they became influenced by the higher critical methods of Biblical study; doubt about the authority of Scripture arose. As a result, the influence invaded our churches and homes. The example has already been given of Dr. Toy who as a devout believer in Scripture became a Universalist after studying the higher critical method.

While I was a seminary student in the Master of Divinity Program and the Doctor of Ministry Program, most of my required readings were by those who accepted the higher critical method of Biblical study. I do not remember a professor who stated that he believed in the inerrancy of the Bible. When Dr. Criswell was President of the Southern Baptist Convention, a group of us students requested that he preach in Chapel and we were told by the administration that Dr. Criswell "was too controversial." But others who were very liberal politically, socially, and theologically were allowed in Chapel. I saw young men graduate from seminary who became leaders in our churches and convention who did not believe in Biblical Authority. Is it any wonder that our homes can be broken asunder when young people have been told by their pastors that the Bible is not true? If the Bible is not true, divorce can break up a home for any cause.

Thank God, we have Presidents and seminary professors who believe, live, and teach the truthfulness and authority of Holy Scripture today. Some of our Baptist colleges and universities have gone to the humanistic and liberal way, but thank God for those who have stayed true to the Book!

All Satan needs is a little crack or foothold.

What a joy it was for me as a teenager to listen to the Old Fashion Revival Hour with Dr. Charles Fuller. What a great man of God and how he loved the Bible. He preached the truthfulness and life changing power of the Word. It would break his great heart, if he were alive today, to know that the great seminary that is named for him no longer teaches the inerrancy of the Scriptures. All Satan needs is a little crack or foothold. I read in a paper the other day where Wheaton, that great college which has stood for the truth so long, now allows alcohol on the campus. All Satan needs is a little opening then and soon he takes over.

We Must Not Allow Satan to Destroy the Home

There is something special about a godly mother. No one can rock a baby, soothe a broken heart or tend to a bruise like a mother. We have had great leadership in all fields of service in America and I would dare say that most if not all got their training at the foot of, and as the result of, praying and caring mothers. As well, along side of these mothers have been hard working fathers whose first priority was the care and protection of their family. I like what history says of John Wesley's parents:

> Samuel and Susanna Wesley were the parents of John and Charles and seventeen other children. The careful Christian training Susanna Wesley gave her children was a strong influence in their lives.[17]

Divorce probably was never mentioned in this home. To abandon their family, would have been the worst of sins for the Wesley family. But today husbands and wives will walk out on their families and have no shame for it. For many, it seems that the marriage vows have very little significance anymore and commitment is a forgotten word. George Barna has this to say about divorce:

> Surprisingly, the Christian denomination whose adherents have the highest likelihood of getting divorced are Baptists. Nationally, 29% of all Baptist adults have been divorced. The only Christian group to surpass that level are those associated with non-denominational Protestant churches: 34% of those adults have undergone a divorce. In the nation's major Christian groups, Catholics and Lutherans have the lowest percentage of divorced individuals (21%). People who attend mainline Protestant churches, overall, experience divorce on par with the national average (25%). Among non-Christian groups the levels vary. Jews, for instance, are among those most likely to divorce (30% have), while atheists and agnostics are below the norm (21%), Mormons, renowned for their emphasis upon strong families, are no different than the national average (24%).[18]

Baptists claim to believe in the total authority of Scripture and yet lead the nation in divorce. What is even more alarming is that 15% of senior Protestant pastors have been divorced.[19]

Three questions about the home must be answered: (1) Is the home worth saving? (2) Can it be saved? (3) What can be done to save the home?. I am going to attempt to answer the first two questions in this chapter while saving the last question for a later chapter.

Certainly, the home is worth saving! The home is the first institution that God put His stamp of approval upon. Out of the home, comes all of the leadership for our institutions upon the earth. The learning process, and values or lack of, begin in the home. A home, that is a godly home, is where mothers and fathers teach children right from wrong (Proverbs 3:1-3). A home where God is in control establishes rules to live by (Proverbs 3:4-6). In a godly home, priority is given to godly instructions and advice (Proverbs 3:7-12). In a godly home, children learn, whether they obey or not, how to live successfully (Proverbs 3:19-26). So much suffering could be avoided if fathers and mothers and children would follow Biblical instruction (Proverbs 4). If husbands and wives would allow God to be in control of their lives and be satisfied with each other, the divorce courts would have to close and remarriage, unless because of death, would vanish (Proverbs 5:15-23).

Is the Home worth saving? Sure it is! My grandparents and mother went through the Great Depression. They knew what it was to be poor, but they had something that many homes with riches today do not have. They had love for each other and a work ethic that with the help of God sustained them. My mother and father separated before I was born, but neither of them got a divorce. My grandparents took mother and me in and provided a home for us. My uncle, who never married, helped support me. One by one, my grandparents, mother and uncle accepted Jesus Christ as Lord. In this home, I learned the meaning of love, security and safety. I learned Christian values and a work ethic which helped prepare me for my own home and family.

God never intended for a mother or father to bring up children by themselves. A home needs a father and mother. Circumstances beyond the control of a parent may come where he or she has to bring up children by themselves. Thank God, for those who are faithful to their children and home. Every person who deserts his or her family, will face the judgment of Holy God. I thank God that my mother did not abandon me. What a joy to hear my own boys say: "Hi Daddy" or "Do you want to go fishing?" What a joy to hear my grandchildren say, "I love you." Yes, thank God the home is worth saving. Satan is out to destroy the home, but he will fail! With the acceptance of living together, homosexuality, humanism, and an attempt to remove God from the scene, things look dark, but God is still in charge. But some will say, "the majority of the homes have left God out." This no doubt is true. It was true in Noah's day, but God won the victory. The home where God rules has the blessings of God upon it, but the home where God is dishonored is doomed to fail. Children today who have Christian parents have a better chance to make it in the world than those who do not. This does not take away that a child is responsible for his actions and must make his own decision to accept Jesus as Savior and Lord. But thank

God for children who have believing and praying parents. Jeremiah knew that nothing was beyond the power of God (Jeremiah 32:17). When I see how the home is in shambles today, I fear for my children and grandchildren. But when I realize how sovereign God has taken care of me, I know He can do the same for my loved ones. But they must want His care and depend on Him (Proverbs 3:5-6). We need parents like Joshua who will stand for what is right no matter what the world says (Joshua 24:15).

Much is said today about a person's rights and freedoms. A careful study of history shows that much blood and many lives have been given in order that we might enjoy the freedom that we have. As a result, those freedoms should never be taken lightly or used irresponsibly.

It is easy to see that Satan is using every means he can to destroy the home. If the satanic forces can claim their rights to destroy the home, surely God's people have a right and obligation to stand against such evil forces. Have we as Christians allowed the schools to remove prayer and Bible reading? Has Satan just blinded us into thinking there is nothing we can do? Do we have to sit idly by and let some pervert teach our children whether it is in the public school or in the church? Just because some judge says that a copy of the Ten Commandments cannot be placed in or on public property, do we have to accept what he says at face value? It seems that we have heard so much about the rights of others until we have allowed our rights to be abrogated. My comments are not intended to be in opposition to law and authority. I am well aware of what Paul says in Romans 13:1-2 and the exhortation of Peter in I Peter 2:13-14. Any home, church, community, or state is in trouble when a few people can decide what is best for the majority. This is exactly what has happened in America. Look at the decisions which have been so detrimental to our freedoms, removing prayer and Bible reading from our schools, and you will see that the cause for the decisions were begun by one or just a few. We are to blame! One man is the reason that the Ninth Circuit Court ruled that the statement "under God" in the Pledge of Allegiance is unconstitutional. If the divorce rate is to be curbed, if the home is to be saved, someone must stand up for the truth.

It is the "Truth" that will set us free (John 8:31-32). Spurgeon tried to warn England about the dangers of falling away from the Bible and the theological leaders scorned him and he died of a broken heart. England is in spiritual decay today. When Dr. W. A. Criswell wrote his book, "Why I Preach the Bible is Literally True", the liberals in the seminaries and churches made fun of him. When in 1979, conservatives began to stand against liberalism in our schools and churches, they were derided by the liberal teachers, preachers, and media. But thank God those conservative leaders stayed the course and our schools and churches are the better for it. But here is a problem today! Many conservative teachers and pastors have a very tenuous view when it comes to divorce and remarriage. As a result, in my opinion, this has caused the church to be partially responsible for the breakup of the home. John in chapter 8 and verse 31 says "if ye continue in my word." He is emphasizing the importance of "staying in" and "with the word." When this happens, "ye shall know the truth, and the truth shall make you free" (verse 32). I am afraid, in order to appease the world, many pastors and churches have left the exposition of the Word and chosen a man pleasing view of scripture.

Chapter VIII

Does the Bible Give Grounds For the Breakup of the Home?

Why is there such an alarming rise in the divorce rate, especially in the church? For those who are not Christians, and hold to a humanistic view of life, it is easy to see why such marriages might fail. But statistics, such as the Barna report, show that the greatest divorce rate is among those who call themselves evangelicals and Bible believers. In their book, Jesus and Divorce, Gordon J. Wenham and William E. Heath give the following reasons for the rise in divorce among evangelicals:

Why is there such an alarming rise in divorce, especially in the church?

> It is our opinion that the rising problem of divorce and remarriage among evangelical Christians today is largely the result of misinformed counsel that arises out of an inadequate exegesis of the biblical data.[1]

What Does Jesus Say In the Book of Mark About Divorce?

It is amazing the reasoning people use when they seek to justify divorce. "Does God expect me to stay in a marriage with an abusive mate?" "My divorce happened before I got saved." Pastors, good and godly men, say, "I will marry the divorced person because it will give me the opportunity to minister to them." It is difficult to understand how one can minister to a person by being disobedient to God's Word! Others will say, "If I don't marry them they will go to a Justice of the Peace or Judge." The Bible nowhere says it is the responsibility of a preacher to marry any one.

When the Pharisees tempted Jesus concerning divorce in Mark 10:3-12, He answered very specifically:

(1) Moses allowed divorce because of the people's hard heart (v. 5)

(2) God never intended for the marriage relationship to be broken (v. 6)

(3) The man who puts away his wife commits adultery against her (v. 11)

(4) The same is true of the woman who puts away her husband and marries another. (v. 12)

It must be noted that Jesus gives no reason or cause that makes it all right for a person to divorce and remarry.

What Does Jesus Say About Divorce In Luke's Gospel? (Luke 16:18)

Jesus is more emphatic in Luke about the indissolubility of marriage than He is in Mark. If a man puts his wife away, he commits adultery (v 18a). Jesus goes even further by saying the person who marries the woman who is put away, commits adultery (v 18b). Humanly speaking, one would think the woman who was put away by her husband would be free to remarry. Jesus certainly does not give her that freedom (v 18b).

What Does Paul Say About Divorce In Romans 7:1-3

Paul uses the same terms that Jesus used in Mark and Luke with reference to marriage and divorce. There are those who argue that these verses have nothing to do with divorce and remarriage. Those who hold to such a view, in my opinion, are reading into the text (eisegesis) rather than giving the true meaning of the text (exegesis).

Does Paul Allow for Divorce and Remarriage In I Corinthians?

Some would say yes, but when compared with Mark, Luke, Romans 7:1-3 and I Corinthians 7:10-11 their theory is very weak.

Paul in verse 10 tells the wife not to depart from her husband. If she does depart, verse 11 tells her to "remain unmarried, or be reconciled to her husband." He says to the husband in verse 11 "don't put your wife away." Now man can come up with his theories about the reasons why a person can divorce and remarry, but he cannot get them from the Bible! If a person separates from his or her mate, as long as there is no remarriage to someone else, there is hope for reconciliation.

What about I Corinthians 7:15 if an unbeliever leaves? Dr. Raymond Brown in the Broadman Bible Commentary answers the question saying:

> The Christian partner in a marriage to a non-Christian is under no obligation to maintain the marriage if the non-Christian partner initiates separation. But the Christian should make every effort to maintain the marriage, which is meant to create harmony, not discord. There is no indication that Paul considers the Christian free to marry again if divorce occurs.[2]

"But wait a minute, I Corinthians 7:27-28 gives all the proof one needs for a person to divorce and remarry", some will say. Let's take a good look at those Scriptures. Verse 27 just simply refers back to what Paul said in verses 10-11. The latter part of what Paul says in verse 27 "art thou loosed from a wife?" refers back to verse 15 when it says, "if the unbelieving depart, let him depart." When Paul says, "If thou marry, thou has not sinned," he is talking to the person he addressed in the first of the chapter. Paul had said, "It is better that you not marry, but if you do it is not a sin." If Paul meant that a person could remarry, (v. 28) he would be contradicting what he said in verses 10 and 11. He would be even more confusing by what he said in verse 39:

> The wife is bound by the law as long as her husband liveth; but if her husband be dead, she is at liberty to be married to whom she will; only in the Lord.

"Only in the Lord" is a great command because we know that the Lord will never lead His children to disobey His Word. Some will say "the Lord led me to marry this person". The Lord may allow, but he will never lead a person to leave his or her mate to marry someone else!

A thorough study of the early church fathers will show that they held to the Genesis view of the permanence of marriage (Genesis 2:24). They saw no biblical grounds for divorce and remarriage. This remained the teachings of the church until Erasmus, in the 16th century, came up with the "exception clause" in Matthew 19. It was not long until Erasmus and his followers were teaching that I Corinthians 7 also allowed divorce and remarriage. When a theologian or pastor begins to take liberties or injects his own opinions into what the scriptures have to say, it will not be long before other changes will occur. Wenham and Heath refutes the Erasmian view by saying:

> We have endeavored to show that this interpretation is quite foreign to the thought of Mark, Luke and Paul who gives no hint that anyone may marry after divorce. All their explicit remarks condemn such marriage as adultery or in Paul's case forbidden by the Lord.[3]

I purposely chose to discuss Matthew 5 and 19 after Mark, Luke, Romans, and I Corinthians. Most conservatives agree very quickly that Matthew 19 gives the right to divorce and remarry because of immorality. Many even will add that I Corinthians 7 also gives that right. But there are a number of problems with the Matthew 19 exception clause and the right many conservatives find in I Corinthians to remarry. First, we must decide whether Jesus changed His mind about what He said in Mark and Luke or did someone else (the church) write what is said in Matthew 19. Secondly, we must determine whether Paul was confused when he made his statements about divorce and remarriage.

When Jesus used the wording, "give her a writing of divorcement" (Matthew 5:31) He was referring to Moses' statement in Deuteronomy 24:1. Moses was protecting the rights of the woman. Up to this time, men could put their wives away for any reason and not provide for them in any way. Malachi 2:14 shows how the husbands of his day mistreated their wives by "putting them away" (divorcing them). Malachi 2:16 shows how God hates their "putting away." Whether a man believes in divorce or not, surely he has an obligation to support his wife even if he puts her away.

The statement sounds good and appears to be logical, but is it scriptural?

Jesus gets mighty tough when He discusses divorce in Matthew 5:32. The man who puts his wife away, except for fornication, causes her to commit adultery (v.32). How can divorcing one's wife cause her to commit adultery? This is a serious charge. In marriage, a woman has her God given natural desires met. To tear her apart from this, leaves her open to the wiles of Satan and the world. Jesus even goes further by saying the person who marries this woman commits adultery. Where is any freedom in the verse to divorce and remarry? At best, some will say a person is free to get a divorce if their partner has committed fornication. Even then, one is hard pressed to find the right to remarry. Some of our best scholars say, "If a person has the right to divorce, he has the right to remarry." The statement sounds good and appears to be logical, but is it scriptural?

Now we come to what is called the "exception" clause. This according to many, clearly gives a person the right to divorce and remarry. But as for me, I have not been able to come to the same conclusion since there is such a change from what Jesus said in Mark and Luke. George A. Buttrick has this to say about the exception clause in The Interpreter's Bible:

> The exception except for unchasity was probably not a part of Jesus' own utterance. It is not found in the Marcan account, which is obviously Matthew's source. That qualifying phrase probably reflects the ethic on which the Christian church had settled when and where Matthew wrote. Jesus did not discuss exceptions and

> permissibilities. He said simply that God had made marriage a sacred unity which must not be broken.[4]

I will certainly agree with Dr. Buttrick that the exception clause in Matthew is not found in Mark. But to say that the church wrote it in Matthew goes beyond my belief. Some like Dr. Ryrie in his book, Meant to Last, states that the exception clause is meant for those who were engaged. That is why, according to some scholars the word "fornication" is used rather than adultery. Their reasoning being, fornication is referring to the unmarried, while adultery is referring to the married. Those who disagree will say that the word fornication (pornea) means all sexual immorality.

When the Pharisees tried to trap Jesus with their questions about divorce, He took them back to the beginning of the home. Let's take a good look at what Jesus said in Matthew 19:4-9.

1. In the beginning God made male and female v. 4
2. Because God made male and female man must leave fathers and mothers and cleave to his wife v.5
3. As a result, they become one flesh v.5
4. They are no longer two, but one v 6
5. Man has no right to separate what God has joined together v 6

Jesus answered the Pharisees very plainly, but they were not satisfied with His answers. It appears from the questions of the Pharisees in verse 7 that they understood Jesus to mean that there was no legitimate reason to dissolve a marriage. The Pharisees used Moses' statements in Deuteronomy 24:1-4 and asked Jesus why Moses allowed divorce. Jesus gave them two answers.

1. Moses allowed divorce because of the hardness of man's heart. He never commanded it!
2. But from the beginning it was not so. Jesus takes them right back to verses 4, 5 and 6.

There are those who say Genesis 2:24 is God's original "ideal for marriage" as if to say the "ideal" cannot be kept. That type of reasoning is not compatible with what Jesus has to say in Mark and Luke.

When sermons are preached, books are written, and seminars are taught that the "exception" in Matthew gives the "innocent" party the right to divorce and remarry, very little is said about Jesus' statement in Mark 10:1-12 and Luke 16:18. When a study is done by those who even go beyond the "exception" and use I Corinthians 7:10-15, they leave out I Corinthians 7:39 and Romans 7:2-3.

Evidently, the disciples were not sure of the "exception" by their response in verse 10. If Matthew 5 and 19 were the only places where Jesus talked about divorce and remarriage, I could see the possibility of divorce and remarriage because of continued immorality. But when I read the passages in Mark and Luke, I do not have the assurance that there is any reason why a marriage can be broken! More and more, I lean towards the theory that Jesus is talking about unfaithfulness before one is married. According to Jewish custom, an engagement could only be broken by divorce. When Joseph wanted to put Mary away privately is an example. In my study of scripture, if marriage can be dissolved any way other than death, it would be because of immorality. Let's say immorality is grounds for divorce and remarriage. If the church just accepted that one cause, the divorce rate would be drastically reduced in this country.

There are two things that I certainly have no problem believing: one is that Jesus did not change His mind in Matthew about what He said in Mark and Luke about divorce and remarriage and secondly, the church did not change the wording in Matthew. In reference to Paul's teaching, we know that Paul was not only a biblical theologian but he was also a systematic theologian. As a result, Paul would not have said divorce and remarriage was all right in one verse and change his mind in the next.

Chapter IX

What Can the Church Do, If Anything, to Strengthen Marriage and the Home?

Whether one looks in the religious or secular field, it is not hard to find materials or statistics which show that the home is in trouble. There are religious and secular counselors, family programs, divorce retreat seminars, and marriage seminars, and yet, the divorce rate continues to rise. One must wonder what is being taught, especially in the religious areas. When many denominational groups meet, concern for the condition of the family is paramount. Words can be pretty, but useless. Too many times, we try to fix problems with band-aids when major surgery is needed.

The Church Must Take Some Blame for the Destruction of the Home

The Roman Catholic Church had to face up to the immorality of some of her priests. Is it possible that this great sin is a result of poor theology and poor biblical exegesis? Let's be careful before we become so spiritual. Have you looked at some of the Protestant groups and even those who claim to believe the Bible word for word? Did you read where one group ordained a homosexual as a priest, or about the evangelist that was arrested for child molestation, and what about the pastor or youth worker who destroyed their home by running off with a church member? Some of these same ministers will move to another church to destroy homes again. Many of the leaders in our churches, especially in the singles and youth divisions are led by people who have been married multiple times. What kind of message are we sending to our young people? Some years ago a couple who was to teach a marriage enrichment seminar said, "Should w tell him, (meaning the preacher) that we just got married again?"

How Has the Church Compromised Biblical Teachings About Divorce and Remarriage?

In seeking to be helpful and redemptive, has the church moved beyond the grace and mercy of God? It is possible for our emotions to cloud the Word of God. If we are not careful, we will begin to ask the same question that the serpent asked of Eve when he asked "Yea, hath God said?" (Genesis 3:1). It is easy to look at circumstances and determine that God will certainly understand the particular condition and make it OK. If it were left up to me, I would agree that a mate who is abused, put out, left for someone else, has every right to divorce and remarry. But you see it is not left up to me. My feelings have nothing to do with what God's Word has to say. Man does not have to give an account to me, but rather to God!

In the case of divorce and remarriage, some churches and pastors just disregard biblical teachings and do what they feel is right. But for the majority of pastors who perform such weddings and the churches who allow the same, they are honestly seeking to be helpful to the broken and hurting families. I can appreciate the care and the concern of the pastor and church who reaches out to the broken and hurting. But a greater concern of mine is this, when the Word of God is abandoned or compromised in this area it becomes easier to compromise when other emotional or hurtful issues arise. Listen to the comments, "I will marry them in order to minister to them, he broke the covenant by his immorality so, she is free, the marriage was not made in Heaven any way, God does not expect me to be alone, God understands that I need someone to help me raise my children." These comments are pragmatic, meaning, that the comments are made in relationship of today's views and values rather than the Bible. When it becomes convenient to change what the Bible says in one place, it is easy to change in other places.

As has already been noted, the early church fathers taught the indissolubility of marriage based upon Genesis 2:23-24. When Erasmus introduced his theory based upon Matthew 5 and 19 called the "exception" clause, the majority of scholars and pastors joined in on this view. This is still the majority view today. It was not long before theologians and pastors began to teach that I Corinthians 7 also gives the right to divorce and remarry. Today, some pastors and theologians will remarry people no matter the cause of divorce. At the same time, many churches allow people to be married in the church who have been married multiple times before. In fact, church members accept and prepare for such marriages as if it were the first one and directly according to the Bible. Is it any wonder that the world has lost respect for the church because the church, in many instances, has lost respect for the truthfulness and authority of the Bible?

The problem of divorce does not end with the lay membership, but extends to the pastors and ministerial staff. Many churches have division today because there are those who want to call pastors and deacons who are divorced and remarried. Recently, at least two search committees have told me of their frustration as they searched for leadership. Yet, many wonder with so many ministers available, "why are so many churches without leadership?" God does still have His standards for pastors and deacons. But what has happened? The Word of God has been abandoned to suit the "changing times." When the Bible in I Timothy 3 says of the pastor and deacon "one wife", it can really mean "one at a time" according to those who want God's qualifications changed. The proponents of the "one at a time theory" say this is the best wording because of the polygamy of the day. This theory will not hold water historically and it certainly is full of holes biblically. Paul certainly knew the customs of his day and he was not accustomed to frustrating those to whom he wrote. Many will use the reasoning that the Greek scholar such and such said, "one at a time" is the correct translation. You know, it was the so-called scholars who said that the world was created as a result of a "big explosion." It was the so-called scholars who said we came from a tadpole. There are those who said because of the structure of the bumblebee "he could not fly." As to scholarship, I was told in Bible School, college, and seminary that the best scholars of that day translated the King James, American Standard, Revised and I have The Bible in 26 translations from the Greek and they all say, "of one wife." Listen to these words from A Commentary Critical, Experimental and Practical on the Old and New Testament:

> Though the Jew practiced polygamy yet, as he is writing about a Gentile church, and as polygamy was never allowed among even laymen, the ancient interpretation that the prohibition is against polygamy in a candidate-bishop is not correct. It must mean that, though layman might lawfully marry again, candidates for the episcopate or presbytery was better to be married only once.[1]

If marriage is a picture of Jesus and the church, what kind of message is being sent to the world when Christians marry multiple times? If the qualifications of pastors and deacons are to be above the standards of the world, how can God's qualifications be broken and such leaders not be disqualified.

A person can walk out of a marriage today for any reason, and little, if anything, is said. Church membership, leadership position and social standing in the community are the same. Since marriage has been so diluted, is it any wonder that the homosexuals are calling for same sex marriages, church membership and leadership? All Satan needs is a little room to work. With respect to marriage, we have gone from no reason to "separate" to the "exception", to "more reasons" to "any reason" and now to the destroying of marriage altogether with "same sex marriages." How did we get in such a mess? The homosexuals are saying the Bible does not condemn their lifestyle. In their view, the Bible does not mean what it says. Listen to the voices of those who say, "We must accept them as they are, we cannot be judgmental and unloving or we will lose them." Where have we heard such reasoning before? When there is no need for repentance, every thing goes. This mentality will lead to the teaching of universalism. That is in the end, every one will go to heaven no matter what one believes.

The following suggestions for the church and her leadership are challenging and in some ways radical. Back in 1979, a group of concerned Southern Baptists recognized that our beloved denomination was drifting away from biblical truthfulness and authority. What has happened since then has caused pain and fracture, but the results for good have been worth it all.

All over our convention, we take pride that the authority and inerrancy of Scriptures are once again proclaimed. Let's stop talking about it and let it be manifested in our homes. Let's get back to the basis of what God's Word says about marriage and the home rather than what the humanists proclaim. It is time for the church to listen to God rather than letting the world set the standards for the church.

Let's begin with the pastor. What can he do to help stop the rise in the divorce rate in the church? He must abide by biblical standards in his own life. He cannot have one set of standards for himself and another for his members. He cannot allow circumstances in his life, home, or community to deter him from God's standards. God's man is to be a pure man (I Timothy 5:22). He is to be a faithful man (I Corinthians 4:2). He is to be a biblical preacher (II Timothy 4:2). When the Word is preached, there will be times when people will rejoice, but there will also be times when people will groan (II Timothy 4:2). There will be times when some will not listen to the truth (II Timothy 4:3). Expound and explain the truth (II Timothy 2:15-16). It is the Word and not the preacher that will change lives (Hebrews 4:12). God has promised that His Word will produce results (Isaiah 55:11). At a conference led by Dr. Johnny Hunt, someone asked him why it was that his church grew so and is blessed by God. He answered, "We hold the standards high and don't lower them." When the biblical standards are held high for marriage, the divorce rate will drop for Christians. Too many of our pastors and churches have no standards for marriage. As a result, our young people get the idea it is all right to run in and out of marriage. But some will say, "If I don't marry them someone else will." Let the someone else do it! They will have to answer to God for lowering His standards.

In addition to expository preaching and teaching to church members about biblical marriage, there should be biblical counseling for every person the pastor marries. Many pastors are already requiring this of those preparing for marriage.

If a pastor will only counsel and marry those who abide by what the Scriptures have to say about marriage, it will not take long for the word to get out. Henceforth, those who do not have biblical grounds for marriage will not seek him out.

God said in Malachi that He hates divorce (Malachi 2:16). Moses allowed divorce, but Jesus said it was never in God's plan (Matthew 19:8). From what God says and what Jesus said it seems only natural that God-called men would want to do everything possible to curb the rising rate of divorce. Let's look at some options for likeminded pastors. What if these pastors, and I know immediately, there will be those who are opposed for every reason under the sun, would agree that they would not perform any marriage ceremony unless there were biblical grounds for such a marriage. In the case of remarriage, only those who had lost their mate by death or those who had lost their mate as a result of continued immorality, would be married by this group. It would be understood that some pastors would only remarry those who had lost their mate by death. It may be that some pastors already have such a plan in action.

In these days of compromise, any church whose pastor stands firm on the teaching of the Bible should be thankful. Since Jesus established the church and died for her, His standards ought to be held high and well known in a community. No church member should ever ask his pastor to do anything, which disobeys the Word of God. This is why, since the church is the bride of Christ, every church should have plain rules and regulations about marriage. These biblical rules should be voted on by the church. This would leave no room for a disgruntled member to get angry when the pastor refused to perform a ceremony that is not according to biblical standards. Furthermore, the church should not allow another pastor or leader to come in and perform a ceremony, which the pastor refused to perform. In my opinion, it is unethical for someone else to do in the church what the pastor refused to do on biblical grounds! "This is too narrow a position for any church to take, " some will say. Friend, the way of the Lord is "narrow." But you can be sure of one thing, when you are abiding in His way, you won't have to worry about being lost or wonder whether you are doing the right thing or not. If more churches in our Baptist Associations would begin to take stands that are biblical, the church would look more like a precious bride. Too many today come to the church for weddings, not because of the spiritual value, but rather for the social convenience. When the church begins, in all areas of her life, to teach that marriage is for one man and one woman until death separates, the divorce rate will decline. Dr. Johnny Hunt in a Sunday message to his people said, "Do away with remarriage and divorce will practically disappear." He is right on target.

Let the emphasis that has been placed in recent years on inerrancy in our schools, literature, and pulpits be placed in the same places about biblical marriages and watch the difference in the divorce rate. We must get away from the Devil's tricks of "you just don't know my situation" or "the times have changed" and "you must realize that we are living in a fallen world." God's word does not change because of situations and the reason the Bible has the only correct way is because we are living in a fallen world. The reason we are in a fallen world is because man was disobedient in the beginning.

If a marriage is going to last, it takes the joining together of two special people. This means people who are committed to the Lord. When a Christian marries a non-Christian, he is being disobedient and disobedience always leads to trouble (II Corinthians 6:14). It is easy to see why marriages are failing by looking at the number of pastors and missionaries who opposed the 2000 Amendment to the Baptist Faith and Message with reference to wives "submitting" to their husbands. Even at the state conventions, arguments put forth against the Amendment were flawed. If pastors and missionaries oppose what the scripture has to say, what can be expected from lay members? In a home where a man and woman are submitted to Christ, and the woman is submitted to her husband, and the husband loves his wife like Christ loved the church, you will have a lasting home (Ephesians 5:21-15).

It is amazing what God will do with pastors who are obedient to Him. Jeremiah was such a man. He was called of God before he was born (Jeremiah 1:5). When a pastor and church take a stand against divorce and remarriage there will be those who cry "unfair and unloving."

I am not talking about taking a stand against individuals, but against a practice that has destroyed many homes because God's word was not obeyed. Was it unfair and unloving that God would not allow Jeremiah to marry (Jeremiah 16:2)? Was God unloving? God's love saw beyond the feelings and needs of Jeremiah (Jeremiah 16:1-3-4).

The church is not a social club. Neither was she created to win a popularity contest! It is amazing how church members, somehow, have the idea that they "own" the church. As a result of such a mentality, they reason that they should be able to do as they please in and around the church building. But when members come to the realization that Christ is the head of the church and as such gives directions to the church, self begins to fade. When a member is surrendered to the Lordship of Christ, he is not going to ask his pastor or church to disobey the teachings of the "Head". The church is now paying for compromising the truth of the Bible. It is one thing to be concerned about those whose lives have been turned upside down, but there must be a turning back to the Bible. Neither pastor nor the church can fix or undo that which has been done in disobedience. When churches band together to teach and model the truth God will bless and there will be positive results. When our young people learn from the homes, pastors and churches that marriage is a life long journey, they will have a deeper respect for marriage and make solid preparations for their own wedding. When individuals recognize that their wedding is a picture of Jesus and the church, if they are Christian, they will want to please Him.

If pastors and churches in an association can agree that the Bible teaches the permanency of marriage, as has already been stated, this will have an effect on an entire denomination.

In 1997, the Louisiana Legislature came up with what is called "Covenant Marriage" and it states:

> We do solemnly declare that marriage is a covenant
> between a man and a woman who agree to live together
> as husband and wife for so long as they both may live.
> We have chosen each other carefully and disclosed to one

> another everything which could adversely affect the decision to enter this marriage. We have received premarital counseling on the nature, purposes, and responsibilities of marriage. We have read the Covenant Marriage Act, and we understand that a Covenant Marriage is for life. If we experience marital difficulties, we commit ourselves to take all reasonable efforts to preserve our marriage, including marital counseling.[2]

Hopefully, more states will follow the lead of Louisiana and seek ways to strengthen and save marriage. I use the term "save marriage" because there are those who are seeking to destroy marriage as we know it today. The papers and news reports were filled with the news that Canada is about to approve same sex marriages. You and I know that nations and states can pass all the laws they wish, but they will never change God's plan for marriage, "One man for one woman for Life." A woman and woman and man and man who seeks to be legitimately joined together is a perversion of marriage and an abomination in the sight of God. The judgment of God is upon any state or nation who condones or passes such an act (Proverbs 11:5-6). Surely, if states are recognizing the danger facing our homes, it is time for the church and her leadership to "stand in the gap."

Chapter X

What Part Does Repentance Play When God's Word Has Been Disobeyed?

"Some people act as if divorce and remarriage are unforgivable." "One sin is no greater than another." "If you think it, you just as well do it." Such statements are usually said without giving much thought to what is being said. I don't know of anyone who believes that divorce and remarriage are unforgivable. There are sins which carry greater consequences than others. Jesus said in Matthew 5:28 that if a man looked, and if that look became lust, he had committed adultery in his heart. It is true that the man had sinned, but he had not physically hurt the woman which would have been a much greater sin. If someone hates me to the point of murder in his heart, it does not carry the same consequences as if he physically kills me!

What Is the Meaning of Repentance?

Repentance means to be sorry for sinning against Holy God. If one is to be sorry, he must admit there is sin. He must admit that God's way is right and his is wrong (II Corinthians 7:10). Repentance means to turn around. Before one recognized his sin, he was walking away from God. Now that he has admitted and confessed his sin, he is walking with God. When a man comes to Jesus, he must admit his sinfulness and throw himself on the mercy and grace of God. His changed lifestyle will show that turn around (Matthew 3:7-8) (II Corinthians 5:17).

When have you ever heard any person who has divorced and remarried say he or she has sinned? During my years of ministry, I have witnessed those who just walked out on their families without any shame or remorse. I have watched those who were guilty live a happy-go-lucky life while the offended party suffered and wondered why things happened as they did. It is natural for a lost person to be unconcerned about his or her actions, but it is not natural for a Christian to walk out on his family and not be concerned. I am glad that I do not have to be the judge as to who is a Christian and who is not, but the Bible is very specific (Hebrews 12:6-8). It is time that the church, for the saved and unsaved, let it be known that they will not be used to make a mockery out of marriage. Specific Bible standards agreed upon by the church and enforced by the church will stop those who just walk out on their families from being married again in the church. It will also discourage those who have not been in church for years from thinking they can use the church just for a social gathering and convenience. It is time that people look at their lives and decide whether it will be God's way or their way (Proverbs 30:12). It must be understood that disobeying God's word is sin. People seem to think that they can break God's rules and then get forgiveness. But in order to get forgiveness, there must be repentance.

Can a Person Repent After He Deliberately Disobeys God?

When I was in seminary, a student asked the theology professor the following question, "If a person remarries and has a living spouse, is he living in adultery or is it an act?" An honest question by some is, "In order to be forgiven, must I leave my second spouse?" Oh, my friend divorce is such a tangled web and so many are hurt and affected by it. I don't know the author of the statement "you cannot unscramble eggs" but he was so right. You cannot undo one wrong by committing another wrong. There comes a time when a person by the grace and help of God must do the best he can in the situation where he is. When a person admits and confesses his sin, he needs to accept the forgiveness of God and get on with his life. Too many, and this is especially true with reference to divorce and remarriage, carry around guilt and want to blame everyone else for their situation. When the church or pastor speaks out against adultery, they want to claim that they are uncaring and unloving. A person who has gone through divorce and remarriage and has truly sought God's forgiveness, in my opinion, would want others to be taught the truths of God's Word. It is very doubtful that the person who gets upset with the church and pastor, because he stands on the Word, has peace and forgiveness in his own heart.

Even when there is repentance, after divorce, can the damage that has been done ever be restored? I really doubt it! Some scars will never be removed until glorification day. A young boy was particularly unruly this class day and the teacher was amazed because he was always well behaved. The teacher learned later that the boy's father had walked out on his family earlier that morning. Is it any wonder that the little boy was unruly? When a young girl finds out that her mother, who is the queen of her life, is leaving for another man and family, is it any wonder that she says, "I will never get married?"

I know that to some I sound preachy, hard and uncaring. I will confess to being preachy and hard, but no harder than what the Book says. But I am not uncaring. However, I will say to you, as I have said to my young people in the past, I would rather that you get angry with me now for telling the truth, than for you to come back later after you have messed up things and say, "Preacher, why didn't you tell me the truth?"

It is easy to say, "you are condemning and judgmental." If a person is lost, he is already condemned (John 3:18). If he is saved, Jesus has removed that condemnation (Romans 5:1). It is not my plan to judge, but you can tell the difference between a saved and a lost person (Matthew 7:16-17). There will be a Judgment for the saved (Romans 14:10) and for the lost (Revelation 20:11-15).

Let's look at how Jesus dealt with those who were caught in immorality. When Jesus met the woman at the well, he told her He could give her living water (John 4:10). Jesus knew that she had had five husbands and was living now with another man (John 4:16-18). This woman did not get angry with Jesus when He confronted her lifestyle. She went and asked others to come see this man who had confronted her (John 4:20). Do you think this woman continued to live in her immorality after she asked, "Is not this the Christ?" (John 4:29) I believe that she had received the "living water." The woman in John 8:6-11 is a beautiful picture of the grace and forgiveness of our Lord. Many people grasp the forgiveness of our Lord, but fail to learn the lesson when He said, "Go and sin no more" (John 8:11). When Jesus met this woman in verse 3, she was living in immorality, but when she left Jesus in verse 11, she was a pure woman because of the cleansing power of the blood (Isaiah 1:18). Praise to His blessed Name!

Revival Would Come If Those Who Disobediently Divorced and Remarried Would First Repent Before God and Ask Forgiveness of Those Whom They Hurt

This may seem like a contradiction since I stated earlier that a person cannot "undo what has already been done." Even after a couple goes through a divorce, there is still hope for saving the marriage. Once remarriage occurs, all hope of reconciliation is gone. This is why, if a person is a Christian, divorce should be the last resort and remarriage should not be an option!

Couples are confused when it comes to marriage, because there are so many conflicting teachings about it. In the early beginnings of this nation, the sanctity of marriage was held very high. But when the law of the land began to liberalize the divorce laws, pressure was placed upon the church to do the same. The result being, a person can get a divorce for almost any reason and can be remarried in most churches without any questions being asked.

Can the trend of easy divorce and remarriage be stopped or at least slowed down? I think the trend can be drastically slowed if we get back to biblical obedience and proper exegesis and exposition in both preaching and teaching.

It is obvious that many Christians have already gone through divorce and remarriage. In addition, there are those who will continue to do so no matter what the Bible, church, or pastor have to say.

It has been stated by many that, "divorce is worse than death". In death, a person can grieve, but in time he is able to get on with his life. The pain and agony, in most cases of divorce lingers, smolders, and festers as time goes on. This is especially true of the partner who has been terribly wronged.

Let's just suppose that a man is immoral and walks out on his family for another woman. He was a leader in his community and church with a fine wife and children. The fine wife is crushed and begins to have questions about her own womanhood. The children begin to have nightmares and wonder what they did wrong in order for their dad to leave. The mother who has never worked outside of the home has to find some kind of job to make a living for her family. The father's only concern is for his new family while his previous family is left destitute. This forsaken mother and her children have every right to be hurt and angry. In fact, it is very difficult for the mother and children not to hate! In time, this father, along with his second wife are convicted of their sin. They both recognize that their immoral relationship which led to their marriage and the destruction of a home was sin against Holy God. They both confess their sin to God and ask and accept His forgiveness. What must they do now? They have hurt and shamed their local church. The witness of their local church has been hurt in the community because of their sin. Remember the words of Nathan to David when he said:

> Howbeit, because by this deed thou hast given great occasion to the enemies of the Lord to blaspheme, the child also *that is* born unto thee shall surely die. (II Samuel 12:14).

Since they have confessed their sin to God, they ought to confess to the church that they sinned. Remember how David confessed his sin to God (Psalm 51:1-3). He also confessed to Nathan that he had sinned (II Samuel 12:13).

Now comes the hard part. If he wants the guilt to be removed, he needs to repent to the wife and children he abandoned. "But suppose they will not forgive him." That will be one of the hard results of disobedience, but he will have shown that he had repented. What can he do if the previous wife forgives him? It will take the grace of God for her to be able to forgive him. If this man really means business, he should help support his previous family. Next he should ask his children for their forgiveness. Most children of divorced parents are the ones who are hurt the most. It must be most difficult when these children have to be torn between their parents. This is especially hard on children when they see a parent showing more concern for another family than for them. When this father goes to his children to ask for forgiveness, he must be prepared for rejection. The children might welcome his request for forgiveness with open arms. Yet, they may not. They may have so much hostility that it will take some time for them to understand and believe that their father is sincere. It must be remembered that these children have been hurt as a result of their father's rejection, but more than that they have seen the pain and agony that their mother has suffered.

Let's analyze what this father's repentance before God, his church, and family can mean. Since this father was a Christian, his sin had to bother him (Psalms 51:3). Repentance was the only way he could get any relief (Psalms 51:4). He knew that he was filthy before God (Psalms 51:2). His joy was gone (Psalms 51:12). He knew he had lost his testimony in the church and community (Psalms 51:13). He could not have a right relationship with his fellow man until he had a right relationship with God (I John 1:9-10). Pride could have kept this man from confessing his sin. He could have done just like many are doing today by saying "he had every right to divorce and remarry." But he would also be carrying the cancer of guilt and continue to live a life of deceit. But what a joy to experience the forgiveness of his loving Lord. This forgiveness does not make his divorce and remarriage right in the sight of God, but it gives him the opportunity to get on with his life.

Now that he has confessed his sin to God, why should he confess to the Church? What business is it of the Church? What every church member does, good or bad, affects the church. Unconfessed sin, by church members is the reason the church is so powerless today. We can have all the programs and all night prayer meetings, but until sin is confessed, there will be no victory (Joshua 7: 10-11). This man as a member of the church is a part of the bride and Jesus demands a pure bride (Ephesians 5:26-27). When this church member deserted his wife and children for another woman, he lost fellowship and his testimony with those around him. That is, he lost fellowship with those members who believe in being obedient to the Lord. The courage and honesty of this man will have a drawing and forgiving spirit from those around him. It will also have an effect upon those who supported and condoned his remarriage. They may begin to think, "If it was wrong for him to abandon his family, it was wrong for us to be a part of it." If the pastor performed the wedding, he may begin to wonder, "If it was a sin for him to marry, it was a sin for me to conduct the wedding." All those who attended the wedding may begin to wonder, "If it was a sin for him, it was a sin for us to attend."

"Wait just a minute," some will say. "What you are suggesting may be all right in an ideal world, but don't you know that we are living in a sinful world?" Yes, I do know that we are living in a sinful world, but I also know that Jesus makes a difference in the lives of His children (Romans 8:5-6). Too many people, including some pastors, act as if the immorality in the world is happening because people cannot live any differently. If man has to depend upon his own strength, this would be true. But for the child of God, this certainly is not true (Galatians 2:20). The man's request for forgiveness in the church will get the attention of those inside and outside of the church. It could spark a revival among those who are in the same boat of divorce and remarriage that he is in. What an awakening when others begin to admit to God and the church that they have been unfaithful to the marriage vows. Those kinds of confessions would make others realize how the sanctity of marriage has been cheapened! Even though forgiveness is granted by God and the church, the previous marriage cannot be repaired, but it might prevent this man and others from being disobedient again. It could very well keep others from destroying their homes. It no doubt could be a wake up call for those who are about to walk out on their families. Most of all, it could cause our young people to recognize that marriage is to be broken only by death. As a result, of one man's confession, I can see young people beginning to study what the Bible has to say about marriage.

Now that confession has been made to God, the church, and the forsaken wife, where does this leave the "put away" wife? Only God knows what is ahead for her. Hopefully, she was able to grant forgiveness when her "former husband" asked for it. If she was able to let go of her anger, bitterness, and hatred she is well on the road to recovery. Someone right quickly will say that she is "free to marry again". Church people are good matchmakers without finding out if it's God's will. If she were free to marry again, who said it was the best for her. Second marriages, according to statistics are more likely to end in divorce than the first. She has already been hurt and does not need to be hurt again. She can go to some of the church singles classes and find her a man. I talked to a man some months ago who did that. He found a woman in the class and now that they are married, neither of them attend church. One young woman was invited to a Bible study and after the study; she was invited to the local bar by the same man. If you take Matthew 19:9a alone, there may be some room for remarriage, but the last half of verse 9 leaves some doubt. When you compare Luke 16:18 and I Corinthians 7:10-11 and Genesis 2:24 you are on the safest ground to say that marriage is not to be broken for any cause.

Can the "put away" wife make it without getting remarried? In her marriage, her physical and emotional needs were met. A young woman gave her testimony that God met her every need after her husband walked out on her. She never remarried, but God's grace was sufficient (II Corinthians 12:9).

"It just isn't fair." This could be the comment of most of us. In this world where sin has done so much damage, what is fair? After he had endured so much was it fair that Moses did not reach the Promised Land (Deuteronomy 34:6)? As you study the life of Job, was it fair for him to suffer as he did (Job 13:15)? Look at Jesus on the cross and tell me what fair is. I just left the home of a mother, who is faithful in her church, as she prepared for breast cancer surgery. Read the eleventh chapter of

Hebrews and explain to me what fair is when you see the suffering of those who died for their faith.

Sure, this mother and rejected wife can live a pure life without getting married again. There are many young women and men whose mates died while they were still young. They chose to live a single life and honored their Lord as they did. There are those whose mates rejected them for someone else, but they remained steadfast as a single person for Jesus. It not only can be done, it is being done. These who are faithful and steadfast are committed to their wedding vows even though their mates are not. Praise God for those who are so faithful when they could have gone the way of the world.

When the world is allowed to invade the church, it is easy to see why God's standards are set aside. This has especially been true with the divorce and remarriage issue. America needs Christians whose influence can be felt in the church and community (Acts 17:6). We need to get back to doing things God's way rather than our way. The word Christian, in most places, has little resemblance of Jesus Christ. If a person is not willing to be obedient to the teachings of Jesus, he has no right to claim His name (Luke 14: 33). This wife who has been rejected by her husband will be able to make it because Jesus will never reject her (Hebrews 13:5-6). She will find special strength in her Lord (Philippians 4:13). The pressures of the world will be great, but she will have trusted the One who has faced every trial she will ever face (Hebrews 4:14-16). Her every need is secure in Jesus (Philippians 4:19). She has been let down by her husband, but her Lord will never forsake her (Psalms 37:25). Since this wife is a Christian, she will find support from her church. At times, she may feel rejected because she is divorced, but in time, her godly walk will even win those who might be suspicious or reject her. As she pours her life into the work of the Lord, healing will take place. Even though she lost her husband, the fact that he admitted his sin and asked for her forgiveness, hopefully will allow her to forgive him.

What a contrast this wife is to those wives or husbands who seek someone else to marry to get even. Their reason being, "if he or she can get someone else, so can I." Many times such decisions are made out of anger and frustration without considering the consequences. Some remarry because of economic reasons. None of the reasons mentioned can guarantee a healthy marriage. In fact, those remarrying for such reasons will most likely be miserable and end up in divorce again. Most of those who marry under such conditions never seek God's will in this matter. Some will even say, "I know what the Bible says." When a couple were about to divorce because of an affair, friends suggested that they go talk to the pastor. Their reply was, "I know what he will say." They did not want to hear the pastor say, "What you are doing is sin!" James has a good answer for such people (James 4:17).

Most divorces come as a result of selfishness. Meaning, "I want things my way." Children are the ones who suffer the most. With lawyers who advertise for quick and easy divorces and judges who have an overload of cases, there does not seem to be anyone who stands up for the children.

In the case of the father who had repented to God, his church, his wife and now his children, what will the results be for the children? Since this is a hypothetical case, our conclusions will have to be based on conjecture. Just how much these children will understand about the father's asking for forgiveness will depend upon their age. If the children are younger, they may respond favorable just to receive the father's attention. As a result of the father walking out on their mother, the older children might have a hard time forgiving and trusting their father. They may withhold forgiveness in order to hurt him. After all, they may reason, "look what he did to mom." "Does he really think we can forget all that he has put us through?" "Where was he when we needed a father?" "What does he think it does to mother when she sees him with another "wife"? "How does he think it makes us feel when we see him at the ball game with his "other children"? Divorce has such tragic consequences, and remarriage just adds to the tangled web.

Because the mother has forgiven her husband and is getting on with her life, hopefully the children, by God's grace, will forgive him also. Even though they forgive him, he can never be the father he should have been. There is no way a father can love and provide for "two families" as he should have for "one"!

Let's look at what forgiveness of their father will mean for the children. First, forgiveness will be like a life threatening cancer that has been removed completely from the body. The relief that comes will be like a boil that is lanced to let out the poison from the body. Secondly, it will allow the children to have, at least, some contact with their father without hatred and hostility. Thirdly, since the father has confessed that he was wrong, hopefully he will provide some economic help for the family. Fourthly, and most importantly, this turn about with their father may prepare them for their own marriage and home. Just how might a broken home and forgiveness be a strength later? When many children see the hatred and hurt caused by divorce in their own family, they determine never to get married. They are afraid that they will end up just like their parents. Because of what some children see in their own parents and their lack of stickability in their marriage, they either decide to live with someone outside of marriage or move from one marriage to another. However, since the children in this story have seen and experienced forgiveness, they might have a different outlook on marriage.

Although it is too late for the father in this story, it does seem by his actions of repentance, that he now understands that marriage is for one man and one woman for life. I use the words "understands now" because it appears that he either did not understand the permanency of his marriage or he was just disobedient. When I see young women and men marry someone who is already divorced with children, I just wonder how much thought they put into what they are about to do? Here is a young person never married, about to marry someone who has already been married; and about to take charge of children who belong to someone else. I doubt seriously that such a person has prayed much, read much, or thought much about what is about to transpire. Marriage has become so tainted and diluted by the world until "sanctity" has very little meaning. There are those who can point to such marriages and show that it can work. That may be true, but it was never God's design in the beginning. I say again, when people say, "until death do us part", they don't fully understand what they are saying or people are just plain disobedient. I think that we as pastors must share the blame for our people not understanding the sanctity and permanency of marriage. My people knew where I stood when it came to divorce and remarriage. All those whom I married were required to attend counseling. I pointed out all the Scriptures that dealt with marriage as a life long journey. I preached that divorce and remarriage were wrong. But I now wonder, did I do all that I could have done? Because there were so many members who were divorced and remarried in the churches where I pastored, did I fail to exegete and expound the Scriptures for fear of hurting or angering those members? Every pastor must come to the realization that those who have disobeyed God's Word cannot undo what has been done. Even if members are hurt or angered, pastors must give a clear message to those who can be helped. It is yet to be seen how the divorce rate will drop when people begin to listen to and obey God's Word. In order to obey the Word, people must understand the Word. This is the responsibility of the pastor (II Timothy 4:1-2).

Let's get back to the children in this story, who have forgiven their father. Because of all that has happened to their home, when these children get old enough to date, I believe they will seek God's guidance in looking for a mate. When that mate is found, I see them searching God's Word together in order that their marriage and home will have the right foundation. When they have finally set the date for the wedding, they will seek godly, biblical counseling from their pastor. The day finally arrives for the wedding. It is fitting that this wedding be in the church. This young couple has kept themselves pure for each other and they are asking the Lord and the church to bless this union. What a picture for Jesus and the church. This young couple will have good and bad times, but their marriage is secure because the correct instructions are being followed.

Humanism would say it is impossible for the events mentioned in this story to happen in our day. In fact, the world would say the events of repentance and forgiveness are unnecessary. You see, the world believes that it is man's right to do as he pleases, no matter who is hurt. But it must be understood that I am talking about Christians and not the world of humanism. Christians are different even though they allow sins to mess up things. The man in this story recognized and admitted that he had sinned. He could not undo all the hurt he had brought to all concerned, but what he did through confession and repentance and the forgiveness that came caused the peace of God to flow in lives again.

Because of liberalized divorce laws, a man or woman can walk out on his or her family by saying, "I don't love you anymore." This just is not right. In some states, a person can get a divorce in three months and be married immediately to someone else. "But that is a person's right," the cry goes up. What about the family that has been destroyed? Don't they have rights also? Someone had better speak up for the family because there are forces in this world that are determined to destroy the family as God intended it to be. Looking at the divorce rate in the church, it appears that the church and her leadership are doing very little to combat those forces seeking to destroy the home.

The Friday, June 29, 2003, Augusta Chronicle Newspaper had the following bold statement by the Associated Press: "Court overturns ban on gay sex." In the same article, Justice Antonio Scalia who voted against the ban wrote:

> The court has taken sides in the culture war," Justice Antonio Scalia wrote for the three, suggesting the ruling would invite laws allowing homosexual marriages.[1]

What a tragedy it is for the majority of the Supreme Court to side with such deviant behavior. We need more men like Justice Scalia who will stand for what is right. We need to put into practice what Paul says in I Corinthians 16:13:

> Watch ye, stand fast in the faith, Quit you like men, be strong.

After the tragedy of 9/11, our country established The Home Land Security Network for our protection. This network is to be made up of the best law enforcement people that can be found. In every area of the country, this group or groups are to be on the lookout for anything or anyone who would endanger our country. Yet, right here in America, there is an enemy which is more dangerous and sinister than any terrorist could ever be. In the Monday, June 30th, USA Today, John Ritter wrote:

> Many conservatives see gay life as deviant, unhealthy and anti-family. But 2000 census data for California found gay couple households and married heterosexuals similar. Gay couples raised an average 2.01 children, compared with 2.08 for married couples. Virtually the same proportions owned homes, with the same $225,000 median value.[2]

Ritter further wrote:

> A Gallup Poll in May found public approval of civil unions at 49% nationally, up from 42% in 2000.[3]

I don't know where Gallup found his information, but if he is anywhere near correct; it is scary. It amazes me that homosexuals do not believe in biblical marriage and yet want to raise children. One must wonder what will happen to children who are raised in such an environment.

In the same USA Today article, there was one leader who spoke up for the family:

> Senate Majority Leader Bill Frist said Sunday that he supported a proposed Constitutional Amendment to ban homosexual marriage in the USA.[4]

The Senate Majority Leader is to be commended for his stand. It has already been said that it would be difficult to get such an amendment passed. Such an amendment would have to be approved by two-thirds of the House and Senate and ratified by three-fourths of the states. It is a shame for such an amendment to be needed but even more of a tragedy is the idea there might not be enough representatives, senators, and states who would vote for such an order. Where are the people of integrity and decency? God give us men who will "watch" for the old enemy who is out to destroy the home. Give us men who will have the backbone to stand for the truth in all areas of our country. Give us men who will stand for that which is right no matter the cost. Under the guise of freedom, our homes are being destroyed from within. Gibbon's book on the *Decline and Fall of the Roman Empire* points out how Rome decayed from the inside.

It is obvious that America will not be saved by the Supreme Court. We need to pray for the Justices that God will direct their decisions. We cannot depend upon our governmental leaders to save America. When we hear of the corruption and lifestyle of many in places of leadership, we are reminded of the Biblical statement that the "blind cannot lead the blind" (Luke 6:39). Praise God for our President and those in leadership who do love the Lord and seek to stand for Him. We cannot depend upon those who want to regulate the one true God to a place along side of the gods of this world. It is a known fact that the homes of America will not be saved by those who want prayer and Bible reading out of our schools. Certainly, those who are afraid for the Ten Commandments to be placed in public places cannot be trusted with the protection of America and her homes. America's hope is in the very God who so many have rejected. II Chronicles 7:14 has the answer. God says there is help, "if my people" will do things my way! My people, indicates ownership. This verse sets in motion the thing which will save America.

Only God's people can humble themselves. It is out of character for a lost person to be humble before God. From this passage, it appears that God's people had become arrogant. Does this hit home in America today? When pastors and churches fail to be obedient to God's standards, they are displaying arrogance. When preachers cater to the membership and the church becomes a social club, that is arrogance. When the divorce and remarriage numbers in the church are as high or higher than those in the world that is arrogance. When you cannot find over half of those who claim membership in our churches, that is arrogance. When the lifestyles of those who are in church are no different than those in the world, that is arrogance.

God is saying, "If you want my help, get your priorities in place." He is also saying, "Get yourself in a position to talk to me." When a person becomes humble, he recognizes he needs help that is far above him. Self is put behind and God becomes center stage. It seems that a crisis must happen before people are willing to bow before and to Holy God. We are in a crisis in America. Our homes desperately need a touch from God.

When there is a true "seeking God's face", there will be a turning from wickedness, and the divorce rate and remarriage will drastically drop. It is wickedness that leads to the break up of homes.

When righteousness reigns, God will open Heaven and give healing. The home is the first institution established by God. If today, mothers and fathers along with their children, I am talking about Christians, would fall on their faces before God in repentance, we would see revival like we have never seen before. Divorce and remarriage would be put on hold for the Christian. If revival breaks out in the home, revival will breakout in the church and will spread throughout our country. If the home truly gets right with God, Satan's crowd could not push through some of the deviant teaching which they are now trying to get passed. There would need to be no Constitutional Amendment to ban homosexual marriages because Christians in the home, church, and community would stop condoning such practices. As a result, I believe you would see homosexuals repenting of their sins. God said healing would come when we meet his conditions. I take Him at His Word. Let's restore biblical standards to the home in order that God's blessings rather than His judgment are upon it.

Chapter XI

The Home Is Badly Battered Today, but God Is Still in the Restoration Business

Many people love to buy old homes and restore them. In many instances, the old lumber is superior to what can be bought today. There are many old homes which have stood the test of adversity. Those who lived in those homes could see the stars through the ceiling and the ground through the floor. They never experienced running water, the toilet was outside, they raised their own food and gathered wood to keep them warm. The children would have so many covers or quilts on them at night until they could barely move. Whoever got up first in the morning almost froze before a fire could be started. There were no lazy people in this home because every person had his particular job to do. Boy, you say, "things must have been terrible back then!" Things surely were tough but this was home life! However, there was love and devotion. No, everyone was not a Christian, but there was a closeness and stickability. Some children were born out of wedlock, but nothing compared to today. When young people started to get married, divorce was not an option. If a man or woman walked out on his or her family, they were not thought well of in the community. Families stuck together, ate together, and worked together. Many of them prayed together and went to church together.

What a far cry from then to now. This is not to say that some who have good houses do not have good homes. However, there are many houses with all the modern conveniences where there is no semblance of a home. "Things" are provided. Physical needs are not lacking. Father takes part at the club and society events, mother has all of the latest fashions and she is a part of the high society group, while the children take part in all of the events of the community and drive the sportiest cars in town. But something is missing. With all of the activities going on, these people do not have time for each other. So much time is spent with others and events, there is no time for home life. In fact, they hardly know each other. Because of such an environment, husbands and wives neglect each other, while the children fail to get the training which should come from father and mother. Is it any wonder that our homes are in trouble?

On the other side of town, we have a different set of circumstances. We have families who can barely make ends meet. They met and in a few short weeks, they were married. They had the glorified idea that love would take care of all of their needs. Because of easy credit cards, they had no problem renting or buying a home. Since both worked, each needed a car. There were many other items, for the home, which were not needed, but since getting them was so easy, why not! But as time passed on, the bills began to arrive. For a while, they were able to make the payments. But in a short while, this bill was behind and the calls for payment began. Suddenly without warning, the wife finds out she is pregnant. They had not planned on this. In fact, they had been very careful and thought there was no way pregnancy could happen. While both of them worked, they could at least keep their heads above water. What will they do now? Who will take care of the baby? Frustration, fear, and anger set in. Pretty soon, the blame game begins.

In both of these homes, one has everything and one is struggling, the stage is set for destruction unless God intervenes.

How Should a Couple Prepare for Marriage?

It is doubtful that young people today would allow their parents to pick a mate for them like they did in biblical times. Genesis chapter 24 gives a beautiful picture of how Isaac received his bride, Rebekah. Although the customs of our day are very different from biblical days, lessons can be learned from the past. Abraham instructed his servant to get a bride from back home instead of where they now lived. The Canaanites were ungodly people (Genesis 24:3). There were three special things about the bride that was chosen: (1) she was very lovely, (2) she was a virgin, and (3) she was a hard worker (Genesis 24:16). I would say that the servant did a very good job in picking a bride for Isaac. Verse 67 shows that Isaac was very pleased with his bride.

Before World War II, in rural America, young people usually grew up in the same community as did their mates. Many of them went to the same school and church. Therefore, they knew their mate's family background and interest. For the most part, they came from the same socio-economic background. When our men and women went off to war and came back, many brought wives from different parts of the states and yes, world. Adjustments had to be made to customs, values, and traditions. Someone has said, "You can take the boy out of the country, but you cannot take the country out of the boy." Love is often times blind to religious, values, places and family differences. Too many times couples jump into the water before checking for rocks and the depth. Before someone leaps, he should consider where he will land. In order, to be a good swimmer, a person must be willing to follow rules and regulations. A person who makes a living by jumping must know the consequences of failure.

Probably the second most important decision in a person's life is choosing a wife or husband for life. The first greatest decision is accepting Jesus Christ as Lord and Master. Unless a person has committed his life to Jesus as Lord, he will not have the resources to share his life with another. It would be interesting to know how many married couples sought God's guidance in selecting their mate. In comparing those that have had a great and lasting marriage to those that have failed, it would be interesting to know what part God had in each!

An article in the July 3, 2003, Baptist Courier, by Sara Horn and Norm Miller of the Baptist Press says:

> Each day in America, more than 3,571 marriages end in divorce. More than 50 per cent of children in public schools live in single-parent homes. Of the nation's children who live apart from their biological fathers, 50 per cent have never set foot in their fathers' homes.[1]

When one reads such articles as this, he is made to wonder if a person should ever attempt marriage. What is so frightening about this article is that many of these 3,571 marriages are made up of Christians. The recent decision by the Supreme Court supporting the rights of homosexuals to privacy makes one ask, "What is next?" James J. Kilpatrick in an article in the July 6, 2003, Augusta Chronicle, asked the following questions:

> What about polygamy? The relationship of a husband and several adult wives is just as consensual as the homosexual conduct just approved. What of incest? Would the sexual coupling of a 40-year-old father with his 20-year-old daughter fall within the "realm of personal liberty which the government may not enter"? What of the call girl summoned to a private room in a reputable hotel? What of laws relating to adultery, obscenity and public "indecency"? What of laws that define "marriage" solely in the context of a man-woman relationship?[2]

If Paul were alive today, he would surely say: "For I would that all men were even as I myself" (1 Corinthians 7:7). Since Paul was a Pharisee, he must have been married in the past. His views about marriage would indicate that his wife had died.

When a mate is being sought, God should be the investigator. The writer of Proverbs 3:5 has some wonderful advice. If it is God's will for a person to marry, surely God will want that person to have a mate of His choosing. Surely, if a person is Christian, his trust will be in the Lord (Psalms 37:3). God wants His child to "delight in Him" (verse 4). If he will, God will give him the "desires of his heart" (verse 4). These promises, I believe, can be to one who is seeking a mate. If people would fall on their faces before God when seeking a mate, God would answer their prayer (Psalms 37:7). When God answers, and brings the couple together in marriage, He will provide strength for a life long journey (Psalms 37:3). The first step in preparing for marriage is committing one's will to the will of God.

Now that a mate has been found, there should be ample time spent in dating in order that each may find out all they can about each other. There was a time, as has already been stated, when couples prepared for marriage and married within their own community. This is no longer true. Years ago, couples not only went to school and church together, but worked together. This gave each time to understand the values, educational and economic situation of their respective families. But someone will say, "We love and trust each other and as a result it does not matter about our background." We love each other in the church, but because of all the sexual abuse in the world, no worker should be put in charge of our children without a background check. Years ago, a church would not have run a background check on a pastor, but they do today. How many husbands and wives have said, "If I had only known what kind of person he or she was before we married?" It may have been "love at first sight," but that sight needs to see beyond and behind the moment. In short romances, men and women can cover up many things which could be detrimental to a lasting marriage. But when couples date long enough, if God has brought them together, He will give them discernment to make the right choice. The statement, "the family that prays together stays together" is good. But I believe that the couple who prays together before they get married will have a better chance of staying together for a lifetime.

From the Counseling Room to the Church House, Is a Good Way to Start a Home

Whatever the age, couples preparing for marriage need a godly pastor who will counsel them before they say, "I do". Even though a couple may be Christians and prepared for marriage, it is good for the pastor to go over with them, God's purpose for marriage. In doing this, the pastor can explain to them the meaning and importance of commitment to each other. In our day, it seems for many, that the word commitment has little meaning. A friend said to me just this past Tuesday, "In the forties and fifties divorce was not an option." He was right because couples were committed to each other. They had problems, but they had the stickability to work through the problems. Nina and I married in 1953 and as I think of the many couples we knew, who married back then, very few of them ever divorced. So, it is imperative that the pastor explains how commitment to one's marriage vows will compliment God's purpose for marriage (Genesis 2:23-24).

Surely, by the time a couple comes to the pastor for counseling, they know if they are right for each other. The main thing, is it God's will? Is this the person one is willing to spend the rest of his or her life with? This is not a question for the pastor to answer, but he can help the couple answer the question. Since the couple has come to the pastor for counseling it is assumed that they are Christians (11 Corinthians 6:14). Now that each has assured the pastor that Christ is Lord in their lives, he can give some biblical helps for the life long journey. The following Scripture verses will be helpful; Matthew 5:31-32, Matthew 19:1-9, Luke 16:18, 1 Corinthians 7:10-15, 1 Corinthians 7:39 and Romans 7:2-3. It is important that the pastor properly exegete these passages to the couple because they will be living in a society which is filled with those who disobey these Scriptures.

A pastor, as counselor, can help those preparing for marriage to cut ties which might adversely affect their marriage. After living with mother and father who have made most of the decisions in the home, up to now, it is a learning experience to leave home. This learning experience will entail starting and providing for their new life together. Many young couples have never been allowed to cut the ties to their parents, because many parents don't know what it means to "butt out". Just as these couples need to know when to cut the ties with their parents, they need to know the same with friends. There is nothing wrong with having friends, but those friends should not interfere with family time. Too many men and women still want to act like singles even after they have married. Satan has used so called friendships to destroy homes.

I have never known of a softball that could cook a meal or greet you at the door with a kiss.

When mates begin to spend more time with their friends than they do with each other, it is time to change friends. The pastor might be able to use historical events to explain the danger of not spending enough time with one's mate.

When couples marry, they may have to give up some of the things which were done while they were single, or at the most, compromise. Examples being: (1) The man who is a sportsman may have to cut back on his hunting, fishing, and ball playing; (2) the wife may have to cut back on her clubs or shopping. People who love and respect each other will know when too much is too much! One man told me, "It was either my wife or softball". He was a smart man so you can decide which he chose. I have never known of a softball that could cook a meal or greet you at the door with a kiss. It is better to have an understanding about these things before one gets married. My youngest son loves softball, but when his twins came along, he knew where his priorities were. Loving his wife and those girls was more important than softball. Such discussion in a counseling session may seem trite, but they may keep a home from being destroyed later. During counseling, it is important to discuss having and rearing children. The responsibility of each parent should thoroughly be studied from a biblical prospective. Too many men have the erroneous idea that it is the mother's responsibility to care for the child. He then expects her to cook his meals, clean house and be a beautiful lover at his every call. Boy, if that is his idea, is he in for a surprise. If he expects all of these things, he had better learn how to wash dishes, change diapers and all that goes with being a husband and father. The tragedy is that we have far too many who get married and have no idea of what it means to be a father and mother. As a result, the lives of two adults are destroyed and children abandoned. If not completely abandoned, the child is passed from one parent to another like a football.

The Three Leading Causes of Homes Being Destroyed Today

Many husbands and wives do not properly communicate with each other. The lack of communication leads to problems with money and sex. Many pastors and counselors hear the same story, "I wish he or she would just talk to me." This is an area where the pastor can really find out a lot about the couple, but more importantly, the couple can learn a lot about each other. It just does not make sense that a couple can talk and plan together while dating and shut each other out after marrying. When counseling a couple, I have them to write down something they dislike about each other. When they finish, I have them to discuss their differences. It is far better for them to discuss such things in the open rather than letting it be a barrier later. Many a mate has gone to bed with anger in his or her heart, while the other mate did not have a clue as to what was wrong. Husbands and wives need to understand that their mate is not a mind reader.

How money is used can cause disaster in a marriage. It is refreshing to counsel a couple who has made wise decisions with reference as to how they will make a living and pay their bills. When I married, it was the custom for the husband to keep up with the bills and see that they were paid. But in this day, when both husband and wife work, sometimes the wife can do a better job of keeping the checkbook balanced while paying the bills. I know one wife who got upset with her husband because she had to pay the bills. Another wife stated, "My husband has a master's degree, but he cannot balance the checkbook." The church treasurer at one church I pastored stated, "Almost half of the checks in the offering plate are signed by the wives." When Nina and I married, we did not have to worry about who would balance the checkbook because we did not have one. These are things husbands and wives should have an agreement about before they get married. The misuse of credit cards has many couples in the divorce court. Trying to keep up with the neighbors or trying to start out where it has taken their parents forty years to get has brought anger and mistrust. Couples who work need to understand that what they have belongs to each other together. When the pastor is counseling couples for marriage, he could help them by discussing the total meaning of I Timothy 6:10.

Problems with communication and money can destroy a wholesome sex life. Many men come to a marriage relationship with ideas about sex that they get from the movies, dirty books, TV, and the Internet. As a result, they think only of themselves and their wife as an object for their own pleasure. Many women come to the marriage relationship with idea that sex is either dirty or a tool to use over their husband. Both views are unbiblical.

When a pastor comes to the subject of sex in his counseling session, he must be discreet and helpful. This is where a godly pastor who has been faithful in his own marriage can be so helpful. I Corinthians 7:5 can be a good starting place when Paul says:

> Defraud ye not one the other, except it be with consent for a time, that ye may give yourselves to fasting and prayer; and come together again, that Satan tempt you not for your incontinency.

The word "defraud" means to keep away, deceive or withhold. When a man and woman are united in marriage and their vows are sealed by the sexual union, they become one (Genesis 24:67). This means that they belong to each other and have no right to be selfish with each other (Mark 10:7-9). The sex act, which was designed for husbands and wives, by God, was not only for procreation, but also for love and pleasure. It is God's way for a husband and wife to show their love for each other in a most intimate way. Husbands and wives are to do everything possible to meet the sexual needs of their mate. This could entail how one puts the other first, their mode of dress, appearance, and helpfulness around the home. Such concerns will make each feel like a king or a queen. When husbands and wives meet each others sexual needs, there will be no reason to allow Satan to cause them to look elsewhere. The wedding rings should say to all, "He or she is mine and no one else is wanted or allowed in this most intimate circle." This is a good time for the pastor to urge the young couple to fight and protect their home against the wiles of Satan. Paul again points out the privileges and blessings of marriage when he says:

> Marriage is honorable in all, and the bed undefiled: but whoremongers and adulterers God will judge (Hebrews 13:4).

When I have the bride and groom sign their marriage certificate, I say to them, "you can't go anywhere tonight without this paper". Married couples don't have to sneak around and feel guilty or dirty when they want to have a love relationship. But God's Word says a man who has sex outside of marriage is a whoremonger and the woman is an adulterer. Where is the shame of broken promises and relationships? Men and women in some circles commit their sin, even while they are married, and have no shame or remorse. But Paul said, "God will judge them" (verse 4). After I preached a sermon on the home, a young man came up to me and said, "You never have to worry about me saying anything wrong to or about your wife." The world should know that husbands and wives belong to each other and woe be to the person who tries to move in on the relationship!

Some Suggestions That Will Help Keep the Home Happy and Lasting

Now that the pastor has gone over the three areas that can cause so many problems in the home, hopefully this couple has learned how to manage the areas discussed. I thank God for the many pastors who take the time and require all those whom they marry to go through extensive counseling. It is the belief of this pastor that many homes can be saved if proper counseling is done before marriage.

There are all kinds of pressures facing the home today. But if the husband and wife are anchored in the Lord, their home can be a place of joy and delight. John has some very encouraging thoughts when he says:

> Now ye are clean through the word which I have spoken unto you. Abide in me, and I in you. As the branch cannot bear fruit of itself, except it abides in the vine; no more can ye, except ye abide in me (John 15:3-4).

When couples abide in Jesus, the divorce court, that is for Christians, will be empty. Sure there are Christians getting divorces, but you can be assured that someone is out of the perfect will of God. People who abide in Jesus will get their directions from God's blessed Word. They will also be on their faces before God asking for His direction. God's children will be helped when they trust their Heavenly Father (Proverbs 3:6-7).

Don't allow the humanistic teachings of the world to invade your home. When troubles come, too many seek the advice of the world. Listen to what God's Word has to say:

> For all flesh is as grass, and all the glory of man as the flower of grass. The grass withereth, and the flower falleth away: but the word of the Lord endureth for ever. And this is the word which by the gospel is preached unto you (1 Peter 1:24-25).

Be sure that you are in a church where the Bible is believed and taught. Every family needs to be under the protection and guidance of a Bible believing church. Families need the fellowship and love of fellow believers:

> And they continued steadfastly in the apostles' doctrine and fellowship, and in breaking of bread, and in prayers (Acts 2:42).

When children come into the home, parents need all that the church has to offer. This is why it is so important to be in a Bible teaching and praying church. Satan is out to destroy the home, but in those homes where Christ is the center and foundation, he is a defeated enemy. Listen to the Word:

> For though we walk in the flesh, we do not war after the flesh: (for the weapons of our warfare are not carnal, but mighty through God to the pulling down of strongholds;) casting down imaginations, and every high thing that exalteth itself against the knowledge of God, and bringing into captivity every thought to the obedience of Christ (II Corinthians 10:3-5).

I am sure that parents in every age would say that their age was a difficult time to raise children. What a blessing it is to see newlyweds grow in the Lord. Difficulties will come, but those who have their faith in the Lord will use those difficult times as stepping-stones for strength. Rather than being driven apart by trouble, it draws them together. They learn together the meaning of sacrifice and stickability. Their homes, though modest, are a castle to them. When God sees fit to send a child to this home, this young couple can understand the Psalmist and his meaning for them (Psalms 127:1-3). This young couple would never dream of destroying their baby (Psalms 139:14). It is a joy to watch a family train their children in the ways of the Lord (Proverbs 22:6). Children in this type of home will not be allowed to run wild (Proverbs 22:28-29).

Proverbs 31 is the picture of a family who loves and respects each other. If a young couple wants a model to follow, here it is. You have a wife and mother who is a pure woman. The Scriptures seem to indicate that such a woman is hard to find (Proverbs 31:10). Today's society as a majority would laugh at someone, man or woman, who is virtuous. But this is not to say that there are no pure, virtuous young people today. Thank God that there are men and women who come to their wedding day and have kept themselves pure for their future mate. Our society needs those who are models for our youth. There are rubies that cannot compare with a pure woman (verse 10). It is no wonder that this mother has the trust and admiration of her family. This is the kind of woman that God would want to be in charge of every home. In such a home the word, divorce would never need to be mentioned. Look at her qualities: she fears the Lord, she is virtuous, she loves her husband, she is a hard worker, she is not selfish, she is a wise planner, she sacrifices, and she knows how and when to open her mouth.

Very little is said about the husband in this story, but enough is said to know that he was well pleased with his wife and children. He loved and respected his wife (Proverbs 31). It is evident that this father and husband was thrifty himself because of the position he had in his community (Proverbs 31:23). The events mentioned in Proverbs point to a loving, growing, stable, and secure family.

It certainly appears that the children in this passage were taught the ways of the Lord by their parents. There are so many children today who do not have parents that seek what is best for them. What a joy to read in Proverbs 31 that the children praised their mother for all of her hard work (verse 28). I believe that the mother in Proverbs 31 had to be a beautiful woman. Add to that natural beauty her lifestyle and you have the beauty queen of the day! Again, let's remember, this is the kind of home God wants each family to have today.

Our homes can be such today! When there is trust in God, purity, sacrifice, working together, respect, and perseverance, that home will stand secure. May revival begin in our homes where love will abound, children will be loved and protected, and the divorce courts will be put out of business. This will become a reality when God's Word is obeyed. Right now, there are husbands and wives who are hurting because their mate has been unfaithful. Children are walking the street unable to get in the house because of selfish parents. A wife or husband, because they have been abandoned by their mate, is about to fall into immorality just to show that "two can play the sin game." No matter the excuse for immorality, it is sin. The home, the pastor, and the church must begin to realize that they cannot compromise with sin and not get hurt.

Chapter XII

What Insights Can Be Gleaned From This Study to Help Stem the Tragedy of Divorce?

When I was ready to build my house, I wanted the blueprints to be drawn by an expert. Different people gave me advice as to how I could cut corners and save money. I even examined some just-built homes and was not pleased with the workmanship. At first, I was disappointed about all of the rules that had to be followed and the many permits that had to be bought before the work on the house could even start. I will not try to name all those who had a part in building my home, but every man, woman, and child who helped was used by God to help at the right time. I must mention the names of Wayne Raiford and Jim Reece. Brother Raiford allowed me to use his builder's permit and brought his equipment and workers to help with the building. He worked right along side all of us. Brother Reece not only supervised the building of my house, but he and his wife, Beverly, did a lot of the work themselves. Brother Reece meticulously chose the subcontractors to build each area of the house. I doubt that he would have been anymore particular with his own house. Sacrifice and tears are a part of the building. My wife, Nina, told me later that after she and Beverly had painted all day and up into the night she would get in the tub and cry because her legs were hurting her so much.

God Has His Blueprint for Marriage

In our study, we have learned that God's way is always the best way. We have also learned that it is natural for lost people to be disobedient (Jeremiah 17:9). In fact, the lost person does not understand the ways of God (1 Corinthians 2:14). Now what about Christians? We have found that Christians are more likely to get a divorce than non-Christians. Is it a matter that Christians don't know any better, or are they just disobedient? As a result of what I have observed over the years as a pastor, student, husband, and father, it is my conclusion that many Christians are outright disobedient, while others are confused about what is right and wrong when it comes to a decision about divorce and remarriage. There are those who are professing Christians who know and understand what God's Word has to say, but yet, disobey the Scriptures. Confusion reigns when the leadership of some churches is made up of those who are divorced and remarried. Especially when that is true of the pastor and deacons. When singles, those who have never married, and those who are divorced, are taught that a person "has every right to remarry," it is easy to see why so many are confused. This is why it is so important that those who teach singles have a healthy home life themselves and properly exegete the Word of God rather than teach the latest humanistic ideas of the world. Those who teach about family life in the Association and State Convention must be those who have been obedient to the Word and will teach others to be obedient.

There Has Been a Historical Decline in Biblical Teaching About Divorce and Remarriage

When man, from Genesis through Revelation, began to cut corners on God's plan, he brought heartache to himself and those around him (Proverbs 16:25); (Revelation 16:4-7). This study, from the beginning to the conclusion, shows the fallacies of following humanistic ideas over God's plan. Paul warns when he says:

> Beware lest any man spoil you through philosophy and vain deceit, after the tradition of men, after the rudiments of the world, and not after Christ (Colossians 2:8).

God knew what He was doing when He established the home with one man and one woman (Genesis 1:1); (Genesis 2:21-22). This historical event in the Old Testament gives vivid accounts of how God dealt with families. Whether one does a study of the nation of Israel, a particular war or of a king, the focus usually turns to the family (Joshua 24:15). It pays for a family to walk in the ways of the Lord. When the family walks in the ways of the Lord, the nation will take notice (Isaiah 30:20-21). Just as God used the family and nation to prepare the way of salvation through His Son, He is using the family and the church to change a sinful people today (Romans 8:28). God has a perfect plan for His people to follow (Romans 8:29-30). His people are provided the resources to finish God's task here on earth both in the home and church (Romans 8:31-34). Satan wants to destroy the home and the church, but in Christ, both are secure (Romans 8:35-39). When a Christian home is destroyed by divorce and remarriage, it is obvious that disobedience is the cause!

It has been stated earlier in this study that the early church fathers taught that marriage was never to dissolve. They based their conclusions on Genesis 2:23-24. Malachi 2:15-17 added strength to their conclusions. As a pastor and father, this study has reinforced my belief that the marriage vows are to be broken only by death.

Erasmus was a contemporary of Luther. He differed with the Church fathers who taught that the marriage vows could be broken by death alone. Erasmus used Matthew 19:9 to come up with what is known as "the exception clause". Most protestant groups, including Baptists, accept this view today. The "exception clause" was further expanded when professors who studied in European schools returned to the seminaries in America with a more liberal and critical study of the Scriptures. Since these professors did not accept the inerrancy of the Bible, it was easy to say there were a number of reasons why a person could divorce and remarry. As a result, students who were taught by these professors came back to the churches and preached what they had been taught. This led to the rise of divorce and remarriage in our churches. This is why I believe the church is partially responsible for the breakup of the home. The alarming factor is that those who claim to be conservative and hold to the inerrancy of Scripture have gone way beyond the "exception clause" to find ways for people to divorce and remarry. Hence, we have pastors and deacons who are divorced and remarried. Since the door has been left wide-open, it is no wonder that we hear of churches ordaining and condoning homosexuality. As one who believes in the inerrancy of Scripture, I must disagree with the exception theory and especially those who go beyond that theory. If Matthew 19:9 were the only scripture where Jesus addressed the divorce issue, I would agree that He teaches that the innocent party would have a right to remarry. That is, if the offending party was living in continual immorality. But when you compare Genesis 2:23-24, Malachi 2:15-16, Mark 10:1-12, Luke 16:18, 1 Corinthians 7:10-15, Romans 7:2-3 with Matthew 5:31-32; 19:3-9, one is on tenuous grounds to say that there is any scriptural reason for divorce and remarriage.

The Church Can Drastically Help Reduce the Rise of Divorce in the Church

The Church must realize that divorce was never a part of God's blueprint for marriage (Genesis 2:23-24). Therefore, if there is no divorce, remarriage is not an option. Pastors need to stop trying to make God's Word say what it doesn't say and explain clearly, what it does say. The following outline is a summary of what the church can do to protect the existing home and prepare others for their future home:

1. Accept God's Word as being the final authority on the home.
2. Pastors must teach the truth about divorce as outlined in the Scriptures.
3. Pastors must have biblical conviction about whom they will marry.
4. Pastors, supported by the church, should require extensive counseling for all who expect to be married by him.
5. The church should have biblical guidelines for all getting married in the church.
6. The church should not allow another pastor to perform a ceremony in their church when the present pastor refused to perform the ceremony on biblical grounds.
7. Single classes, marriage seminars or retreats should be taught by those who have been obedient to their own marriage vows.

8. Hopefully, biblical stands, proper exegete, and exposition of truths about divorce and remarriage will spread in the Association, the State Convention, the Southern Baptist Convention, and all Christian groups.

Since Barna's research found that Baptists are at a critical state when it comes to the number of divorced, it is high time to change that figure. Just think what can happen if, from the local level to the national level, we start obeying God's blessed Word. It hurts, but it is true that the divorce and remarriage rate is where it is because the church has sought to please its members rather than God! It is my prayer that Baptist pastors and churches will turn their concern for the home to the One who has the correct blueprint. Many pastors and churches have always been faithful and obedient to the Word. Southern Baptists at the 2003 Pastor's Conference put the emphasis on strengthening and saving the home. It may be that God can use Baptists to call other groups back to a biblical understanding of what God expects of the home.

If God Says Something Is Wrong, His People Had Better Believe Him

Beware of any man who seeks to alter the Word of God (Psalms 119:89). Disobedience has its reward (Numbers 32:23). God gave man the choice to be obedient or disobedient (Galatians 6:7-8). Anything that is contrary to the will of God is sin. When divorce and remarriage are mentioned, some are quick to say, "One sin is no greater than another." But in the sight of man, some sins have greater consequences than others. This is certainly true of divorce and remarriage. It is doubtful that many people contemplating divorce ever think about the number of people that will be affected. If there are children involved, they are the ones who suffer most (Lamentations 5:7).

Is divorce a sin? If a person studies the Word of God and takes a look at what divorce has done and is doing, he must conclude that it is a sin. What about the "innocent" person? It is always easy to blame the other person. It must be understood that sin affects us all (Matthew

5:45). It is the belief of this writer that divorce will begin to subside when people recognize what an enemy it is.

In this study, it has been pointed out what could happen in this country if those who have gone through divorce, and especially those who have remarried, would admit that they have sinned and ask for God's forgiveness. Asking for God's forgiveness would send a spiritual shock wave through this country. Revival would come to our churches and the devil and his crowd would take notice.

Oh, how America has drifted since 1620. Times were hard and it would be inaccurate to say that everyone in that day served God. But from 1620 to the early 1940's-1950, times were different. It was and is exciting to study the development of this country. Whether studying about the sacrifices of Roger Williams, the wilderness journeys of Daniel Boone, those who gave us our Constitution, or the many who fought for our freedoms, most came from homes of stability and stickability. These people knew right from wrong. The drifting and erosion of morals and virtues had begun way before 1960, but things were hidden. Yet in our day, man has bought into "the lie" that everyone has a right to do as he pleases (Proverbs 12:15; 21:2); (Judges 17:6). Divorce has become so accepted until people don't look at it as being a sin. "But surely Christians know better," some will say. However, when you see pastors and churches condoning divorce without any regards to what God's Word has to say, what can you expect? I hope this study will be challenging enough to make people come back to God's Word (Jeremiah 6:16).

I don't want to sound like a pessimist, but if God's men don't take a stand against the moral decay in our nation, we are inviting God's judgment. The lack of morals and integrity in one's own marriage leads to further decay in the church and community. You can't expect a husband or wife who is immoral in his or her home to be moral in other areas of life. What is this saying to the world? No wonder we have those who say, "If that is Christianity, I don't want anything to do with it." When people of the world hear that the wedding being held in the church, is the second, third or even fourth time for the couple, what will they think?

Some may be angered by my conclusions, but I trust they will abide by what the Bible has to say (Ephesians 4:26). As for me, I must be faithful to my calling (Ezekiel 3:17-18). I am well aware that Ezekiel was a "watchman over the house of Israel." But I also believe that God's man is just as responsible today when he is called as Ezekiel was (Hebrews 13:17). My calling is not from man, but God and it is to Him that I am accountable (11 Timothy 4:1-5).

The home can be saved, but it has a difficult road ahead. We have family groups today who are asking people to sign petitions stating their opposition to same sex marriages. Others are calling for a Constitutional Amendment, which would recognize marriage as being between one man and one woman. I thank God for these groups speaking up for the family. You and I know that the problems causing homes to be destroyed come from hearts that are not right with God (Proverbs 30:12). While some groups are trying to save the home, others are asking politicians to take a stand for abortion and homosexual rights. Years ago, a politician would not have dared to take such a stand. But today, it is terrible what some will do for power and money. The home will be saved when people are willing to admit that God's way is right and man's way is wrong.

Quite often, you will hear people say, "I wish we could go back to the old days." I certainly would not want to trade my indoor plumbing for the "old days." Nor would I like to trade my central air and heating for the old pot bellied stove. But I would love to see us get back to the time when families were close. It would be good to take time to sit on the porch and visit. It would be great to get back to the time when the marriage vows were taken seriously. It is so easy to forget "for better or worse until death do us part." It would be good to read in the paper "ways to strengthen the family" rather than advertisements for "cheap divorces." I pray the day will come when our states make it difficult to get a divorce rather than making it easier.

In order for the suggestions made in this study to become a reality, pastors and churches must be willing to "pay the price." If a person lives for Jesus, he will be hated by the world (11 Timothy 3:11-12). Don't expect the world's praise when you stand for Jesus (Luke 6:26). One of the lowest times in Peter's life was when he denied his Lord (Luke 22:60-62). It is my sad observation that many pastors and churches have mishandled the Word when it comes to marriage. Thank God, for those pastors and churches who are true to the Word (Jeremiah 3:15). When a pastor has been true to the calling of God, he can stand before the judgment seat of Christ satisfied (Jeremiah 17:16).

There are those who will say, that my suggestions will destroy the church if accepted by pastors and churches. I disagree strongly. In fact, the church will be strengthened. I am well aware that many in our churches are divorced and remarried. Many of these have already asked for God's forgiveness and are getting on with their lives. Those who have not asked for God's forgiveness need to do so. There are many who have been divorced and remarried who are greatly used by the Lord. Problems arise when people have leadership positions in church and teach that divorce and remarriage is not a sin. Such leaders are not being true to God's Word and as a result will lead others to make the same mistakes.

The church must reach out to those in love, who have had the heartache of divorce. When there is remarriage after divorce, the church must minister to those families. It is one thing to minister to families; it is another to condone that which is sin. If there is to be forgiveness, there must be repentance of all sin, no matter what it is called.

Man Has a Right to Protect His Home

If the admonition of Exodus 21:22-24 were followed today, I wonder if we would have the number of divorces and remarriages in our land? If the man, who abuses his wife, suddenly realized that he would spend time in prison for such actions, would he continue his abuse? If the woman of the street or any husband taker understood that the wife would thin her hair, would she be as apt to commit such a wrong? If the husband who comes in after a night of immorality, suddenly found out that his wife would present him a crown made from the frying pan, would he be as eager to go out on the town? If the man who steals a wife had to look over his shoulder or be careful that he did not meet her husband, would he rethink their affair? Someone will scream, "that sounds like an eye for an eye and a tooth for a tooth." Maybe husbands and wives should take better care of their eyes and teeth! The rings on the fingers of a husband and wife should signify, "**private property, no trespassing allowed.**"

It is my prayer that anyone who is about to leave his or her family will read Genesis 2:23-25 and also read their marriage vows together. If immorality has invaded a home, before there is a divorce, I trust that the husband and wife will read the book of Hosea together. But someone will say, "I can't forgive him or her for such a sin." Praise God, Jesus didn't say, "I will not forgive." When a pastor or church is about to condone someone who walks out on his or her family and expects the church to be pleased, hopefully they will read Malachi 2:11-17. If the divorce and remarriage epidemic is to be halted, God's Word must be obeyed. The following Scriptures should be studied carefully: Genesis 2:23-24, Matthew 5:31-32; 19:3-12, Mark 10:1-12, Luke 16:18, Romans 7:1-2 and I Corinthians 7:10-15.

Men and women must stop looking for excuses and loopholes to get out of their marriage and into another. If a person is about to breakup his home and another, he must recognize this as sin. By God's grace and strength, his home can be spared and he will not have to live with the guilt of destroying another home. Where divorce and remarriage has already happened, claim I John 1:9-10 and I John 2:1-2. I am well aware that we are living under grace and not under the law. But Exodus 20:14 still means the same today as it did when it was given. Jesus came in order that the law might be fulfilled (Matthew 5:17). Because of God's grace, men and women can stay out of the divorce court (Romans 6:1-4).

Hopefully the materials presented in this study will be accepted with an open mind. Study the suggestions carefully and decide if they have merit. Study the Scriptures given carefully and determine if your view of marriage, divorce and remarriage is based upon God's Word. In your own view, is the church partially responsible for the break up of the home? Don't just say yes or no. Give your own reasons why you disagree or agree. If marriage is to be a picture of Jesus and the church, can remarriage be such a picture unless as a result of death. It is easy to say, "God knows my situation and understands." The classic statement by some is, "My sins are covered by the blood and whether it is divorce, remarriage, or whatever, I am forgiven." But this does not give us the right to disobey God's guidelines. Dr. J. Vernon McGee gives a great definition of the act of salvation and living the salvation when he says:

> Now let me put it like this: justification is an act; sanctification is a work. Justification took place the moment you trusted Christ--you were declared righteous; the guilt was removed. Then God began a work in you that will continue throughout your life. I believe in instantaneous salvation, but sanctification is a lifelong process. In other words, justification is the means, sanctification is the end. Justification is for us; sanctification is in us. Justification declares the sinner righteous; sanctification makes the sinner righteous. Justification removes the guilt and penalty of sin; sanctification removes the growth and power of sin.[1]

Chapter XIII

When the Storms Come, Call Upon the Peacemaker

When I had my last physical, I received a notice from my doctor that my glucose was 168 and that I should come in for another test. My doctoral studies in ministry had taught me very little about glucose. I had the option of obeying my doctor or ignoring his request and going on with my life as it was.

At the appointed time, I was in my doctor's office for another blood test. This time my glucose was 108. The nurse instructed me to go and eat breakfast and return in two hours for another test. This test showed that my glucose was 126. The nurse felt that the lab had made a mistake in the beginning, but she wanted the doctor to talk with me.

The doctor really got my attention when he said: "You really don't want to fight this disease.

My doctor assured me that my glucose was normal, but because my triglycerides are high, I should be careful about what I eat. I did not like what he suggested: "Stay away from white bread, rice and sugar." He explained how keeping my glucose normal would keep me from becoming a diabetic. My doctor then made a statement that got my Attention: "You don't need to fight that disease."

The choice is mine. I can eat anything that I might desire and run the risk of becoming a diabetic or I can leave off some foods and live a normal life. I am aware that for many diabetes is hereditary. I have seen so many precious people suffer from this dreaded disease. It can cause blindness, kidney failure, inability for sores to heal, and heart failure. I know of a man who burned his feet when he stepped on hot coals because he had no feeling in them. There are many diabetics today, with medical help and more importantly, with God's help, who are living productive lives.

It is Time for Man to Take Responsibility for His Actions

What does my visit to the doctor and his suggestions about my eating habits have to do with the break up of the home? Just as I have the choice of eating or not eating the proper foods for my well being and health, so does a man and woman have the choice of doing what is right to keep their marriage and home in tact.

It would be incorrect to expect a person who is not a Christian to abide by biblical standards the same as a person who is a Christian. Yet, many who are not Christians have a profound respect for biblical guidelines. If this is true of the person who has not surrendered his life to the Lord Jesus, surely the person who has will seek to follow His directions.

Man outside of the Lordship of Jesus Christ has a diseased heart (Jeremiah 17:9). When man fell in the garden, Satan became his master (II Corinthians 4:3-4). It is natural for man to follow his master (I Corinthians 2:14). It is Satan's plan for a man to forsake his wife even though he promised to be faithful to her. Satan is delighted when children are forsaken or passed from one parent to another like a basketball. Satan loves it when a home is destroyed, when a husband or wife is left heartbroken and children are scarred for life. Satan does not care when a husband or wife tries to care for the children alone. Many are doing the best he or she can, but this was never God's way of building a home. God will give grace to those who seek to live by and follow His plan. Because man does not know God, does this mean that he is not responsible for his actions? He certainly is responsible (Romans 1:18-32).

How can people who say they love the Lord get so far out of His will? How can two who prayed together before they married, and pledged before God and man that they would live together until God separated them, turn their backs on their vows? It is not logical to say such is the will of God. Two people committed to God and to each other have at their request grace to get through any problem and to face any circumstance. Somewhere along the way, Satan is allowed to be in control. Paul, in the seventh chapter of Romans, points to the tremendous struggle between the old and new natures. When a man is saved, he receives a new nature, but this does not mean that the old nature is destroyed. When Jesus comes in, He gives His child all the tools for living a victorious life. Listen to what Paul says in Galatians 2:20.

> I am crucified with Christ: nevertheless I live; yet not I, but Christ liveth in me: and the life which I now live in the flesh I live by the faith of the Son of God, who loved me, and gave Himself for me.

But, you know, tools that are not used will become rusty and useless. Christians have the Holy Spirit to guide them in all truth. The Bible is the Christian's handbook and prayer is the open line to God through Jesus Christ. What happens to a book when it is not used? It becomes forgotten and useless. What good is a telephone if it is never used? Many homes have different versions of the Bible, commentaries by the best authors, and devotion books that could inspire the most mundane person. But, too many times, couples wait until trouble comes to find solutions to their problems by searching for answers in the Bible. The writer of the book of Hebrews shows how a person must be in tune with God if he is to understand His Word (Hebrews 5:11-14). If a person hasn't been obedient to God's Word when things were going well, how will he listen to God when problems arise (Hebrews 5:11)? Understanding and obedience come by feasting on the strong meat of the Word and not by drinking milk (Hebrews 5:12). It is natural for babies to drink milk, but they don't understand what is going on around them (Hebrews 5:13). Even before a couple gets married, if their lives are committed to the Lord, they have a knowledge of the Bible and prayer. As a result, they are strong in the Lord and they will have discernment about things which might try to disrupt their home (Hebrews 5:14).

My son tried to call me the other day on my cell phone, but failed because I had left my phone at home. The phone was in good working condition and my son had dialed the correct number. The problem was with me! My mother had fallen and could not get up. Had my son and daughter-in-law not gotten to my mother, she could have been seriously hurt. It was naturally my fault because I had been careless. It is easy to get too busy to pray. Many couples who began their marriage with a tremendous prayer life, let things take the place of prayer. Suddenly, God was no longer allowed to give directions in their home. Just little things began to drive a wedge between their relationship that at one time was so special. Harsh words rather than love notes were passed around. Doing things and going places together was no longer an enjoyment. People at church began to notice the coldness. Before long, both dropped out of church and the dreaded words "I don't love you anymore" were heard. At the urging of friends, the couple agrees to pray about their problems, but prayer itself becomes a problem. It is sad, but true, they have forgotten how to pray. II Chronicles 7:14 gives a beautiful example of what happens when God's people pray. The person who prays this prayer must have an intimate relationship with the father. He must humble himself. A person cannot expect God to answer one who is arrogant and self-willed! Answered prayer comes when a person faithfully wants God to intervene in his life (Luke 11:9). A marriage that is in trouble cannot be helped until the cause of the problem is brought out in the open. Many times couples blame each other. Neither is willing to admit fault. Most of the time, when trouble comes, both are at fault. You can be sure, somewhere in the situation, the old enemy, the devil, has raised his old ugly head. The problem could have started with a word, an action, or just neglect. No harm was meant, at first, but little by little Satan stimulated the action or actions. If there is to be forgiveness and healing, there must be confession and repentance. Just to say "I am sorry" is not enough. Repentance means stopping and turning away from whatever has caused the fracture (1 John 9-10). It is so tragic that many families are missing the blessings of our Lord because they do not know how to pray (James 4:2-3). When trouble comes to the home, Satan can actually fool couples into believing that it is God's will for them to divorce and remarry, but this is a lie of the enemy (James 1:13-14). Man must realize that disobedience is a sin and that sin will destroy (James 1:15). God gives us healing in our homes (II Chronicles 7:14).

Fractures Can Be Mended

David in Psalm 37:3-5 says:

> Trust in the Lord, and do good; so shalt thou dwell in the land, and verily thou shalt be fed. Delight thyself also in the Lord; and he shall give thee the desires of thine heart. Commit thy way unto the Lord; trust also in him; and he shall bring it to pass.

What great promises these are and they can be applied to the home. God gives to each member of the home, especially husbands and wives, the choice of having a home blessed by God or one destroyed by Satan.

Chapter XIV

It Is Time for the Home to Be the Home

It is no surprise that many homes are in trouble. A check of military records will show a marked increase in the divorce rate since the war began in Iraq. Pastors and writers are sounding the alarm with reference to what is happening to the modern home. Only families who are suddenly up rooted by war can understand the stress on a wife who suddenly has to become the father and mother in the home. While the father fights for his country, he has to fight the stress of guilt for not being home to be with his family. It is easy for those who are safe and secure in their family to say "the military families made the choice to serve." Many who signed up for the military, although they knew the possibility, never expected to be on the battlefield. But what a ripe field for Satan to attack. Look at the family where both husband and wife work. Suddenly there is a new arrival to be nurtured. It is no real problem in deciding whether to stay home or use a sitter. Right! Before long, there are ball games, church programs, and time for mom and dad. But suddenly, there is no time for mom and dad. The bolts and screws of the home begin to loosen. Bible reading and prayer are soon neglected. Satan soon points out that Sunday is the only time the family has together. Church is put on the back burner. Ball games on Wednesday nights are more important for the children than prayer meeting and mission programs. Satan is ready to land the knock out blow because he is giving the directions for destruction. When Bible reading, prayer, and the church were considered out-dated, Satan became the intruder. No family that forsakes God's direction is safe and secure. In fact, such a family has a sandy foundation. When the foundation is removed, the house comes tumbling down!

Obedience to God's Word Will Save the Home

The Pharisees of Jesus' day were much like the humanistic teachers of our day. They wanted to please the crowd even if their teachings were in conflict with the Bible. These teachers were familiar with what the Old Testament taught about marriage and divorce. But just like today, they wanted the scriptures to mean what they wanted them to mean! The Pharisees were acquainted with the teachings of Shammaie and Hillel. Shammaie taught that a person could get a divorce for any reason, while Hillel taught that a person could only divorce as a result of adultery.

The Pharisees tried to trap Jesus by using what Moses taught about divorce in Deuteronomy 24:1-4. Jesus in Matthew 19:8 lets the Pharisees know that He does not agree with Moses. Moses was honest in his teachings, but Jesus let them know that this was not God's way in the beginning. In trying to help hurting people put their lives back together, many good teachers and preachers have made decisions with reference to divorce based upon emotions rather than the Bible. Frank E. Gabelein has a good study on Matthew 19:3-12 in the Expositor's Bible Commentary, pages 410-419. Zondervan Corporation, Grand Rapids, Michigan is the publisher.

Erasmus (1466-1536) was a theologian, author, and teacher. He was ranked as the greatest scholar of the Renaissance.[1] It has already been stated that Erasmus coined the phrase "exception clause" in Matthew 19 which is still being followed by many today. Erasmus was a theologian and a humanist. As a theologian and a catholic, he knew that marriage, according to catholic teachings, was a sacrament. Because of this teaching, he knew, divorce and remarriage was an anathema. He wanted to be true to the scriptures and the church, but he was a humanist. Does this ring a bell for our day? "I believe the Bible, but in this case there must be an exception." Erasmus wanted what was best for man. Man and his feelings and needs were the important issues. Erasmus could see change everywhere. The dark ages were gone. Man had emerged as his own master and new opportunities were everywhere. The dogma of the

Roman Catholic Church was challenged resulting in the Protestant Reformation. A study of church history will give an overview of the many denominations and their different methods of biblical interpretations. Erasmus felt that he found the cause whereby a person could divorce and remarry by what Jesus said in Matthew 5 and 19 about fornication. Thus you have what is called the "exception clause or cause." In his Annotations on First Corinthians, Erasmus gives a more detailed study on divorce. For a more detailed study, get Gordan J. Wenham and William E. Heths' Jesus and Divorce by Paternoster Press, Waynesboro, Georgia. It must be understood that Erasmus was not trying to disobey scripture, but rather trying to harmonize man's decisions with scripture. We are on solid ground when man's decisions are based on scripture, but the hill becomes mighty slippery when he tries to make scripture fit his decisions.

I am sure that there are many good ministers who honestly feel that they are in the right when they marry some who have been divorced. If a person has been mistreated, abused, cheated on, or left, surely that person has a right to a better life. I certainly would agree that a person deserves better, but I would not agree that the Bible should be changed because of the conditions mentioned. God is love and His grace is ever near. But, His love and grace do not condone disobedience to His Word!

The following comments of the great New Testament Professor Dr. Frank Stagg are very interesting:

> The debate will continue among interpreters as to whether Jesus took the side of the school of Shammaie against that of Hillel or that He disallowed divorce altogether. It is at least clear that in going back to creation, He affirmed unambiguously that God's intention for marriage is fulfilled only in the life union of husband and wife, not to be dissolved by divorce. In terming the marriage union God's Act of joining two together, Jesus did not say that some marriages are not of God's making and therefore, may be dissolved. There

> may be "marriages" which God has not made, but this passage does not authorize us to dissolve any marriage on the claim that God did not make. There are commitments and obligations in every marriage which may not be removed without damage to all concerned. The word rendered unchastity (Porneia) is usually translated "fornication," and it may denote premarital unchastity, Etymologically the term refers to the sale of one's body in sexuality. Thus for a time at least, porneia designated either prostitution or premarital unchastity whereas moicheuai designated adultery, illicit sexuality within and against marriage. The two words came together to be used interchangeably. Whether porneia in Matthew retains its early meaning or not is uncertain. If so, the "except clause" refers to premarital unchastity making possible what today would be called annulment. In Jesus' time it was called divorce, for even betrothal was legal (and often financial) contract which could be broken only by divorce.[2]

It is refreshing to read after a scholar like Dr. Stagg and sense his honesty with passages of scripture that are interpreted differently by many. He looks at the passage and the wordings and explains to the best of his ability what the passage, as well as, the words meant in the days of Jesus and today. He is not dogmatic nor does he try to change the meaning of the passage to satisfy a particular group.

In conclusion, as ministers and teachers, let's do all that we can to save our homes. Let's be faithful to our own marriage vows and let Satan know that he is not going to destroy our own home. Let's allow the scriptures to speak for themselves and not allow humanism or circumstances to cause us to change what the text means. We must recognize, as Barna points out in his research, that divorce is at an epidemic state in our world. We must admit as ministers, as churches, and states, that we are part of the problem because we have liberalized what God's Word has to say about divorce!

What can I do if I am about to get a divorce? First of all, are you a Christian? If you are, get your answer from God's guidebook. Read the following scriptures: Genesis 2:23-24, Malachi 2:11-17, Matthew 5:31-32, 19:1-9, Luke 16:18, I Corinthians 7:10-15 and Romans 7:1-3. Take your problem to the Lord in prayer (Hebrews 4:14-16). Talk to your pastor and let him guide you. Hopefully, he will be able to guide you through the scriptures in making the correct decision. If you are not a Christian, you need to accept Jesus as your Lord (Romans 10:8-10). When you accept Jesus as Lord, you will begin to understand His teachings in the Bible (I Corinthians 2:14). "But, what am I to do if I have already gotten a divorce," some will ask? Again, if you are a Christian, be obedient to the scriptures (I Corinthians 7:10-11). If you have already divorced and remarried, confess it to the Lord and let Him give you peace and healing (I John 1:9).

The other day, I heard a little boy say, "My daddy has left home and I miss him so." How tragic to hear the statement, "It was better for the children that we separate." When will parents recognize that such a statement is untrue. Children need both parents! How tragic to hear on the news or read in the paper where a husband or wife has taken their life and the lives of their children because separation has occurred. I am aware that many will disagree with my conclusions, but if one home can be saved, if one child can keep his parents, if pastors will honestly and prayerfully study together the scriptures mentioned, I believe my time will have been well spent.

ENDNOTES

Chapter IV

[1] H. D. M. Spence and Joseph S. Exell, The Pulpit Commentary, Volume 1 Genesis Exodus (Grand Rapids, Michigan: Wm. B. Eerdman's Publishing Company, 1983) 107.

[2] The Rev. G. F. Maclear, A Class Book of Old Testament History, (Grand Rapids, Michigan: Wm. B. Eerdman's Publishing Company, 1959) 97.

Chapter V

[1] George Barna, 1999 Survey (Glendale, CA)

[2] Rev. C. I. Scofield, Hosa (New York: Oxford University Press, 1945) 922.

Chapter VII

[1] Everett Edgar Sentman, ed, Daniel Boone (Lake Bluff, Ill. The United Educators, Inc., Publishers, 1966) B 270. Copyright © The United Educators, Inc.

[2] Dale W. Jacobs, ed, The Western Frontiers, (The World Book Encyclopedia, Chicago, World Book, Inc, 2000) Volume 21, 232.

[3] We The People: Center for Civic Education: (Calabasas, CA, 1999) 53. Reprinted with permission: Center for Civic Education. Calabasas, CA

[4] The American Legacy, The United States Constitution and Other Essential Documents of American Democracy: (Calabasas, CA: Center For Civic Education, 1997) 5.
Reprinted with permission: Center for Civic Education. Calabasas, CA

[5] Merle Burke, United States History The Growth of Our Land (Chicago: American Technical Society, 1957) 320.

[6] Ibid 310.

[7] Richard Layman, American Decades 1960-1969: (Detroit, Michigan: Gale Research, Inc., 1995) 835.

[8] Ibid 835.

[9] The World Book Encyclopedia, Volume 9, 239.

[10] Timothy Keesee and Mark Sidwell, United States History for Christian Schools: (Greenville, SC: Bob Jones Press, 1993) 77.

[11] William J. Federer, American's God and Country, Encyclopedia of Quotations (St. Louis: Amerisearch, Inc. 1999) 164.

[12] Ibid 4.

[13] Ibid 52.

[14] Ibid 323.

[15] L. Russ Bush and Tom J. Nettles, Baptist and the Bible: (Chicago: Moody Press, 1980) 239.

[16] Webster's New World Dictionary, Elementary Edition, 1966.

[17] B. K Kuiper, The Church In History: (Michigan: Wm. B. Eerdmans Publishing Co., 1951) 350.

[18] Barna Research Group, CA: December 21, 1999.

[19] Ibid

Chapter VIII

[1] Gordon J. Wenham and William Heath, Jesus and Divorce (Waynesboro, GA: Paternoster Press, 1984) 17.
Reprinted from Historical Drift: Must My Church Die? By Arnold L. Cook, Copyright © 2000 Used by permission of Christian Publication, Inc.

[2] Raymond Bryan Brown, (Nashville, The Broadman Bible Commentary, I Corinthians 7 Volume 10, 1970) 331.

[3] Ibid 151.

[4] George A. Buttrick, The Interpreters Bible, Matthew Volume 7, (Nashville, Abingdon, 1951) 480. Used by permission.

Chapter IX

[1] Rev. Robert Jamison, Rev. A. R. Fausset and Rev. David Brown, A Commentary Critical, Experimental and Practical on the New Testament, Volume VI, I Timothy, Grand Rapids Michigan, Wm. B. Eerdmans Publishing Co., 1961) 487.

[2] Louisiana Family Forum, Baton Rouge, LA

Chapter X

[1] Editorial, Augusta Chronicle, June 29, 2003, 3a.

[2] Editorial, USA Today, June 30, 2003, 3a.

[3] Ibid 3a.

[4] Ibid 3a.

Chapter XI

[1] Sara Horn and Norma Miller, Baptist Courier (July 3, 2003) 1.

[2] Editorial, Augusta Chronicle, July 6, 2003, 3a.

Chapter XII

[1] J. Vernon McGee, Through The Bible With J. Vernon McGee, (Volume IV, Matthew and Romans, California, 1942) 681.

Chapter XIV

[1] Ibid Volume DE, E197.

[2] Frank Stagg, General Article Matthew-Mark (Broadman Commentary V 8, Broadman Press, Nashville, Tennessee 1969) 188-89.

BIOGRAPHICAL SKETCH

Dr. Eleazer Benenhaley
6 Sunset Circle
North Augusta, SC 29860
(803) 279-3546 Home

OBJECTIVE:
I am available as Supply Pastor, Revivals and Bible Studies, Beginning June 5, 2005

BIRTH:
September 21, 1934

MARITAL STATUS:
Wife: Nina
Sons: Clayton, Wilbur and Timothy

EDUCATION:
Sumter County Schools: Elementary and High School
Clear Creek Baptist School, Pineville, Kentucky, 1958-61, Certificate
B.S., Cumberland College, Williamsburg, Kentucky, 1965
M.Div.,Southwestern Baptist Theological Seminary, Wake Forest, North Carolina, 1971
D.Min.,Southern Baptist Theological Seminary, Louisville, Kentucky, 1979
Did further graduate study at Eastern State University, Richmond, Kentucky, 1965

CALL TO THE MINISTRY:
Ordained as a deacon by the Long Branch Baptist Church, Sumter, South Carolina, 1953
Licensed to preach by the Long Branch Baptist Church, Sumter, South Carolina, 1955

Ordained to the Preaching Ministry by the Riverside Baptist Church, Four Mile, Kentucky, 1961

CHURCHES PASTORED:

Pastor of a mission established by the Hosman Baptist Church, Four Mile, Kentucky, 1959

Associate Pastor of the Riverside Baptist Church, Four Mile, Kentucky, 1960

Concord Baptist Church, Flat Lick, Kentucky, 1960-68

Siloam Baptist Church, Windsor, North Carolina, 1968-72

Long Branch Baptist Church, Sumter, South Carolina, 1972-81

Sweetwater Baptist Church, North Augusta, South Carolina, 1981-2002, Retired after 21 years

Went to Silvercrest Baptist Church, Augusta, Georgia the next Sunday and just finished three years as interim.

DENOMINATIONAL SERVICE:

Member of the General Board, Kentucky Baptist Convention, 1966

Moderator of the North Concord Baptist Association, Barbourville, Kentucky, 1967-68

President of the Pastor's Conference, Santee Baptist Association, Sumter, South Carolina, 1978

Member of the Missions Committee, Santee Baptist Association, Sumter, South Carolina, 1979

Moderator of the Santee Baptist Association, Sumter, South Carolina, 1980-81

Program Chairman for the Aiken Baptist Minister's Conference, 1982

Director of Evangelism, Aiken Baptist Association, Aiken, South Carolina, 1983. During this time the first Master Life Program was conducted in the association. This was a first for the State of South Carolina conducted in the association.

Wrote lessons for Discipleship Training, Southern Baptist Convention, 1993

Was Chairman of the Missions Committee and Church Extension of the Aiken Baptist Association, Aiken, South Carolina

Moderator of the Aiken Baptist Association, 1999-2000

Member of the General Board, South Carolina Baptist Convention, 1988-92
Member of the Committee on Committees, South Carolina Baptist Convention, 1993
Program Committee of the South Carolina Baptist Convention, 2002-04

OTHER MINISTRIES:
Taught School at the Flat Lick Elementary School, Flat Lick, Kentucky, 1965-68
Taught Biblical History at the Martin Technical College, Williamston, North Carolina, 1972
Coached football at Flat Lick and won the county championship, 1967
Was a member of the Advisory Council for the Sumter County Schools, 1980

OTHER ACCOMPLISHMENTS OR AWARDS:
Received the President's Medal as the student most likely to succeed from the Clear Creek Baptist School, 1961
Honorary Member of the Delta Epsilon Chi Honor Society of the American Association Of Bible Colleges
Authored two books, Moulded Clay and The Holy Spirit Leads Beyond Confusion

All one has to do today is pick up any religious book or magazine, listen to sermon topics, notice the number of seminars and counseling sessions on the family to know that our families are in deep trouble. The question is why?

George Barna has reported that families are dpidemically being destroyed by divorce. The tragedy is that those who call themselves conservative are more likely to get a divorce than those who claim very little religious background. Although there are many different types of Baptist, Barna points out in his study that Baptists are at the top of the list when it comes to those getting divorced.

As a Southern Baptist pastor for nearly fifty years, I am alarmed at the number of members, as well as pastors and religious leaders in my own denomination who take a very humanistic world view of divorce and remarriage.

If those who conduct seminars, counselors, pastors, and denominational leaders have a humanistic world view of marriage rather than a biblical world view, how can they help curb the rise of divorce? It seems, that is to me, that the problem is having bandaids applied rather than radical surgery.

Years ago, in our seminaries and in denominational areas, the scriptures began to be compromised when it came to the permanency of marriage. As a result, this compromise was accepted by many pastors and brought to our churches.

www.ingramcontent.com/pod-product-compliance
Ingram Content Group UK Ltd.
Pitfield, Milton Keynes, MK11 3LW, UK
UKHW020141250726
13967UKWH00002B/788

9 781425 186432